TEACH YOU

Lotus 1-2-3
for Windows

Lotus 1-2-3 for Windows

(to Release 4)

David Royall

Hodder & Stoughton

A MEMBER OF THE HODDER HEADLINE GROUP

A catalogue record for this title is available from the British Library

ISBN 0 340 60067 5

First published 1994
Impression number   11 10 9 8 7 6 5 4 3 2
Year   1999 1998 1997 1996 1995

Copyright © 1994 David Royall

All rights reserved. No part of this publication may be reproduced or transmitted in any form or by any means, electronic or mechanical, including photocopy, recording, or any information storage and retrieval system, without permission in writing from the publisher or under licence from the Copyright Licensing Agency Limited. Further details of such licences (for reprographic reproduction) may be obtained from the Copyright Licensing Agency Limited, of 90 Tottenham Court Road, London W1P 9HE.

Typeset by Multiplex Techniques Ltd, St. Mary Cray, Kent
Printed in Great Britain for Hodder & Stoughton Educational, a division of Hodder Headline Plc, 338 Euston Road, London NW1 3BH by Cox & Wyman Ltd, Reading, Berkshire.

CONTENTS

Introduction		1
1	**Getting started**	3
	1.1 Aims of this chapter	3
	1.2 What is a spreadsheet?	3
	1.3 Hardware and software	6
	1.4 Computer needs	7
	1.5 Operating systems	7
	1.6 Processor types	8
	1.7 Disk drives	8
	1.8 Screen types	9
	1.9 Printers	10
	1.10 The keyboard and mouse	10
	1.11 Data storage on disk	12
	1.12 Computer memory	13
	1.13 Menus	14
	1.14 Installing Lotus 1-2-3 for Windows	14
	1.15 Getting started	16
	1.16 Chapter summary	17
2	**The basics of spreadsheets**	18
	2.1 Aims of this chapter	18
	2.2 Getting started	18
	2.3 Columns and rows	20
	2.4 Moving around the spreadsheet	21
	2.5 Entering text	23
	2.6 Correcting errors	25
	2.7 Entering numbers	26
	2.8 Entering a formula	26
	2.9 Saving your work	27
	2.10 Printing your work	29
	2.11 Erasing data from a spreadsheet	32
	2.12 A new spreadsheet – sales performance	32
	2.13 Asking for help	36
	2.14 Chapter summary	37
3	**Menus, printing and filing**	38
	3.1 Aims of this chapter	38
	3.2 Changing the style of your spreadsheet	39
	3.3 The menu structure	41
	3.4 Saving a file	42

3.5	Expanding your spreadsheet	44
3.6	Relative and absolute cell addresses	48
3.7	Using windows	51
3.8	Fonts, presentation and printing	53
3.9	Chapter summary	57

4 Statistics and graphs — 59

4.1	Aims of this chapter	59
4.2	Reading the indicator	59
4.3	Entering statistics	60
4.4	Good spreadsheet practice	63
4.5	Some new functions	66
4.6	Creating a bar chart	67
4.7	Changing the graph type	75
4.8	Release 1: graph insertion	76
4.9	Customizing the spreadsheet	77
4.10	Chapter summary	80

5 Style and presentation — 81

5.1	Aims of this chapter	81
5.2	Styles for data	81
5.3	Date formats	83
5.4	Naming ranges	86
5.5	Summarising the formats	88
5.6	Protecting ranges of cells	90
5.7	Presenting text	92
5.8	Search and replace	94
5.9	Producing graphs in a spreadsheet	96
5.10	Chapter summary	99

6 Dates and decisions — 101

6.1	Aims of this chapter	101
6.2	More practice with formats	101
6.3	More on manipulating dates	103
6.4	Copying and moving ranges	105
6.5	The @IF function	107
6.6	Relative and absolute formulae	111
6.7	Chapter summary	115

7 Lotus 1-2-3 database — 116

7.1	Aims of this chapter	116
7.2	Setting out a database table	116
7.3	Entering record details	118
7.4	Sorting the records	119
7.5	Sorting using macros	121

	7.6	Enquiring and extracting information from a database	124
	7.7	Further work with a database	135
	7.8	Tracing commands for macros	136
	7.9	Chapter summary	138

8 More on graphs and charts — 140
    8.1 Aims of this chapter — 140
    8.2 More on bar charts — 140
    8.3 Multiple bar charts — 144
    8.4 Changing the perspectives of your graph — 147
    8.5 Stacked bar chart — 148
    8.6 The pie chart with some annotation — 150
    8.7 Line graphs — 154
    8.8 Scatter graphs or XY graphs — 158
    8.9 Chapter summary — 160

9 Three-dimensional spreadsheets — 161
    9.1 Aims of this chapter — 161
    9.2 Looking at multiple sheets — 162
    9.3 Setting up the first sheet — 164
    9.4 Copying between sheets — 166
    9.5 Entering three-dimensional formulae — 167
    9.6 Building up a history — 169
    9.7 Summarising the sheets — 171
    9.8 Adding a fourth dimension — 173
    9.9 Chapter summary — 176

10 Sample exercises — 177
    10.1 Aims of this chapter — 177
    10.2 Selling soft toys — 177
    10.3 Arnold's fish bar — 179
    10.4 An electricity bill — 181
    10.5 Calorie control — 182
    10.6 Employee sickness — 186
    10.7 Price lists for a transport company — 187
    10.8 World weather chart — 188
    10.9 Car burglar alarm explosion — 190
    10.10 League tables — 191
    10.11 Hayley computer services — 193
    10.12 The rapid cook microwave company — 195
    10.13 Council house survey — 197

Glossary — 199

INTRODUCTION

Teach Yourself Lotus 1-2-3 for Windows is an introductory guide for anyone learning how to use the Lotus 1-2-3 spreadsheet package for the first time. It is ideal for people who know little or nothing about computers or spreadsheets as well as those who are familiar with both but want to learn how to use this Windows-based spreadsheet.

Teach Yourself Lotus 1-2-3 for Windows

- Takes readers through simple step-by-step practical activities.
- Explains the underlying principles behind what is happening.
- Contains numerous illustrations throughout showing what users can expect to see on their screens as they work through the package.
- Encourages good spreadsheet practice while conforming to the Windows style of performing actions.
- Contains comprehensive references that will prove invaluable once the basic skills have been learnt.
- Contains many exercises offering many suggestions as to how spreadsheets can be applied as well as serving as a way of further developing skills.

You should work through the book in the chapter sequence set out as each chapter is a progression on the previous one.

The book itself is written with screen dumps from Lotus 1-2-3 Release 4. Those readers who are Release 1 users can also get the full benefit of the book because, where appropriate, explanations are offered where Release 4 differs in operation to Release 1.

1

— GETTING STARTED —

1.1 Aims of this chapter

This chapter gives an outline of what the Lotus 1-2-3 for Windows spreadsheet is, what it can do and how you should prepare your computer for its use.

There is also an explanation of some computer terminology that may be new to you. It will help you get started and ensure that you have what is needed to be successful in using this Lotus product.

1.2 What is a spreadsheet?

A spreadsheet is the electronic equivalent of an accountant's ledger; a large piece of paper divided by vertical columns and horizontal rows into a grid of cells. The name derives from the spreading of the organisation's accounts on a sheet of paper and the user can directly enter numbers, formulae or text into the cells.

Screen Dump 1.1 shows what an empty spreadsheet might look like. The top part of the screen holds various menus and icons that will be used throughout the work you do. The spreadsheet is headed [Untitled] and the spreadsheet working area is made up of a grid of lines on a white background. Your opening spreadsheet screen may differ from this if you are using a different version of the package.

LOTUS 1–2–3 WINDOWS

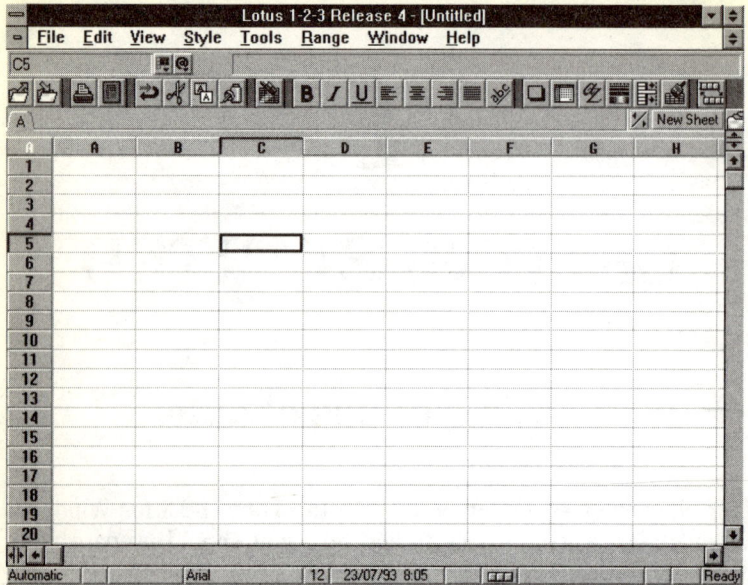

Screen dump 1.1

There are letters along the columns at the top and numbers in rows down the left side of the spreadsheet working area. The section in the middle of the blank area which is outlined in black is referred to as a cell. Each cell is identified by its co-ordinates, like a map reference or point on a graph. The highlighted section here is at C5, i.e. *column* C and *row* 5.

Use your mouse to move from cell to cell.

Click on cell B1, type a number (e.g. 4) and press the **Enter** Key. Click on cell C1, type a number (e.g. 6) and press the **Enter** Key. Then click on A1 and type =B1*C1 and press the **Enter** Key. Cell A1 displays the number you typed in cell B1 multiplied by the number you typed in cell C1. Type a different number in cell B1 or C1 and press the Enter Key. The number displayed in cell A1 will automatically change.

Note that you need to precede a formula with = or +.

The spreadsheet effectively becomes a screen-based calculator capable of being printed or displayed as a graph.

As a "tool", accountancy is by no means the only work for which spreadsheets can be used. Some examples of the power of spreadsheets are:

1 What if? analysis

Any figure can be changed at any time and the new results will automatically be shown. Thus a "What if?" analysis might be: What if sales were to increase by 10%? The spreadsheet can calculate this easily. This facility of being able to recalculate formulae quickly makes spreadsheets a powerful, useful and popular analytical tool.

2 Goal seeking

Some spreadsheets are used in order to seek goals. For example, spreadsheets can be set up to depict the sales and costs of a business where a model is set up to determine at what price profits will be maximised.

3 Graphing

In this instance, the spreadsheet is used to represent tables and figures in the form of graphs.

4 Storing records of information

A spreadsheet can be used to hold records of information such as details of costs accumulated for a specific job. Such information can be altered quickly and can be used as the basis of a contract tender or for price determination. This type of application is often referred to as database management. Using the Lotus 1-2-3 spreadsheet as a database manager will be covered in this book.

In practice, spreadsheets will be used for a combination of the above. Spreadsheets are flexible modelling tools which can be readily adapted for many jobs involving repetitive numerical calculations.

Some other examples of their use are:

- Financial plans and budgets can be represented as a table, with columns for time periods (e.g. months) and rows for different elements of the plan (e.g. costs and revenue).
- Tax, investment and loan calculations.

- Statistics can be displayed, such as averages, standard deviations, time series and regression analysis. Many in-built statistical functions are available in Lotus 1-2-3 for Windows.
- Merging branch or departmental accounts to form group (consolidated) accounts. This involves merging two or more spreadsheets together.
- Currency conversion – useful for an organisation with overseas interests.
- Timetabling and roster planning of staff within organisations or departments.
- In an educational establishment – the recording of class lists, attendance, student marks.

You will probably think of many more potential applications as you work through the book. Lotus 1-2-3 for Windows is a product developed by a company called Lotus Corporation and incorporates three standard applications of spreadsheet, database and graphics. You will soon appreciate that the uses of spreadsheets often combines these three applications.

1.3 Hardware and software

Hardware refers to the physical components of a computer system, while software refers to the programs that are used to give instructions to the computer. Both are needed if the computer is to achieve anything at all.

Software for a computer will come in many forms; essentially there will be an operating system which will come with the computer system, and applications software which you normally buy as extra. Lotus 1-2-3 for Windows is an example of applications software. This product operates in the Windows environment, so you will also need Microsoft Windows software, which is an extra application used with an operating system.

When the machine is switched on, the computer will need some instructions about how to operate the computer system, hence the term operating system. Different computers will have varying kinds of operating systems, which needs to be considered when you are buying applications.

When choosing hardware, you will need to make decisions on such issues as how much hard disk space you will need and the quality of your printer. When selecting software, you are making decisions about what you want your computer to do for you.

1.4 Computer needs

There is now a large range of computer types on the market from which you can choose. Use of this Lotus package tends to be associated with a microcomputer, in other words, a computer that stands by itself and allows one person to sit at a keyboard and operate it. However, there are other types of systems, such as networks and multi-user systems on which you will find Lotus 1-2-3 for Windows being used. If you are buying Lotus 1-2-3 for Windows, you must know which type of system you will be working with.

It is important to bear in mind that older machines will not be able to run Lotus 1-2-3 for Windows because they will not have the memory capacity to cope and will not be able to run Windows.

1.5 Operating systems

Although all computers appear similar from the outside, they may well have different operating systems. An operating system is the language that any particular machine has to work with, in much the same way that different peoples of the world communicate in different languages.

Most microcomputers use the operating system MS-DOS (Microsoft Disk Operating System). However there are different versions of MS-DOS. The different versions have come about because computers have advanced over the years with new and more powerful devices, and changes in the operating systems have been required for the new devices to be operated.

Increasingly the operating system OS/2 (Operating System 2) is being used. This has the added advantage over MS-DOS in that many 'jobs' can be executed at the same time. For example, while the computer is printing, an operator can get on with something else without any slowdown in speed. Alternatively, it will allow operators the facility of being able to work on a number of different packages at the same time from one machine.

Network systems require a different operating system again because there will be a number of different machines all working from a common system (normally called a file server). The network operating system will, for example, need to administer all machines using the same software package and a single printer.

With such a range of systems, it is important that before you embark on purchasing a copy of Lotus 1-2-3 for Windows, you check with your supplier that the version of Lotus 1-2-3 for Windows you are purchasing matches the machine and operating system you are intending to use it with.

1.6 Processor types

Part of the computer's hardware is called the processor. All computers need such processing devices as they form the main attributes of a computer system. Over the last few years such processors have become more sophisticated and more powerful.

Not all software packages will run on all processors; so, again, you need to be careful that the software purchased is correct for the machine you have. It is not for a book like this to discuss the varying processor types nor is it necessary for you to know all about them in order to be able to take full advantage of this Lotus package. However, you will need to know what kind of processor you have if you are going to purchase software. Most dealers will be able to identify this by the model of machine you have.

1.7 Disk drives

Getting a computer with the correct disk drives is important. On microcomputers you normally find two types of disk drive, a floppy disk drive and a hard disk drive.

A hard disk normally comes already installed in your machine and cannot easily be removed. It is capable of holding very large volumes of data and the software which is used to manipulate the data.

A floppy disk drive is used to store data on removable small disks. When you receive software, it normally comes on such floppy disks. You will then need to copy the data on to the computer's hard disk – a process called installation. Clear instructions on how to carry this out will come with the software. Such drives typically require disks of one of two sizes; 3.5 inches or 5.25 inches. When buying software, you will need to advise your supplier as to what size of floppy drive you are using to install your software.

Some machines are equipped with both sizes of drive. Floppy disk drives are also needed for backing up data as a precaution against loss of data.

For both types, the amount of data that can be stored will vary from device to device. Hard disks normally store from 60 megabytes upwards, while floppy disks store 1.4 megabytes. In practice, if you are a Windows user, you should have far more disk storage than 60 megabytes.

It is often difficult to appreciate what a megabyte of data actually is, but to give you some idea, a book of this size, if converted to computer data, would fit onto a 1 megabyte disk. When software is purchased, it will normally come on a number of floppy disks with most Windows-based commercial packages taking in excess of 5 megabytes of disk storage. Remember, apart from the software package, your computer will also have to store all the data generated by the software.

1.8 Screen types

At first sight it may seem that one screen on a computer is very much like any other. However there are now many variations. There is first of all the straight choice of colour and monochrome. Many portable computers and notebook computers will only have a mono display.

All new machines will have full graphics capabilities. Older computers will vary in their ability to display graphics. Lotus 1-2-3 for Windows will require such graphics capabilities to operate.

1.9 Printers

You will almost certainly want to print out spreadsheets and graphs. Not all printers will necessarily be able to do this. Printers will vary in speed of print, quality of print and paper width (usually 80 column or 132 column width). Also, not all printer types are capable of printing graphs.

Here is a list of the main types of printer available and a brief description of what they can achieve.

Ink Jet printers. These offer high quality at a low cost. Colour inkjet printers are now becoming cheaper and are an attractive option.

Dot matrix printers. These are in common use but are being replaced by ink jet machines for low budget users. A 24-pin printer will print with greater definition than a 9-pin printer. Matrix printers will also produce graphics output.

Laser printers. These give the best output. They work rather like a photocopier, and can produce CRC for publishing. They are expensive, however, and cannot print carbon copy form.

Whatever kind of printer is purchased you need to make sure that Lotus 1-2-3 for Windows is able to send data to that printer for printing. In practice, it is fairly unlikely that you will select a printer that Lotus 1-2-3 for Windows is unable to cope with. You will be able to use any printer that is classified as Windows compatible.

1.10 The keyboard and mouse

Most keyboards are fairly standard. Before starting, examine your keyboard to determine the whereabouts of the following:

Number pads. On most keyboards there are two sets of number keys from 0 to 9; one set above the QWERTY letters and the other as a number pad to the right side of the keyboard. The reason for this is that some users prefer to use the number pad on keyboard in the same way they would use a standard calculator. If you want to use the number pad you will need to set the Num Lock 'on' when doing so.

Function Keys. These are especially programmed to perform certain functions. On most keyboards they are either along the top or grouped together on the left-hand side. Each key is labelled F1, F2, F3 etc. You will, in time, find some of these very useful when using this Lotus package.

Insert, Home, Page Up, Page Down, Delete, End. These exist on most keyboards and, along with the function keys, offer ways of taking shortcuts. These keys will perform different functions depending upon the package in use. Lotus 1-2-3 for Windows makes full use of these keys.

Arrow keys. These often appear as separate function keys on keyboards. If they do not, then you will have to use the ones that appear on the number pad.

* (Multiplication). This appears above the number 8 key near the top of your keyboard. It is used in order to avoid confusion with the conventional symbol for multiplication '×'. Similarly, / (forward slash) is used for division. So, 8*4 means 8 multiplied by 4; 8/4 means 8 divided by 4.

Ctrl (Control). This will always be used in conjunction with another key. For example, holding down the Ctrl key and pressing the character 'C' (referred to as Ctrl+C) is used in the Windows environment for copying information.

Alt. This is used in a similar way to the Ctrl key in that it is pressed simultaneously with other keys to provide a variety of other facilities. For example, Alt+F4 is used to quit Lotus 1-2-3 for Windows.

Esc (Escape). This key operates rather like a function key and is often used, as is the case in Lotus 1-2-3 for Windows, to 'back track' on a sequence of events or to 'undo' an activity.

~ (Tilde). This is a special key used for the more advanced features of 1-2-3. It is worth checking its whereabouts on your keyboard.

PrtScr (Print Screen). This allows you to 'dump' a copy of the screen to your printer or to the Clipboard. The Clipboard is a part of your computer's internal memory that can be recalled at a later stage. **PrtScr** prints a text screen only.

/ (Forward slash). This key is important when working with 1-2-3. Remember to distinguish it from \ (Back slash). The forward slash is used as a division symbol in most applications.

Getting to know your keyboard is important. However, you will find that if you are new to computing, this will take quite some time and you will need to be patient. Progress can be slow when you are learning a new package such as Lotus 1-2-3 for Windows and discovering your keyboard at the same time.

Computers now come equipped with a pointing device called a mouse, which offers an alternative to the keyboard for performing actions. The mouse is moved around on a flat surface, often on a mouse mat, and interacts with a small cursor that appears on the screen. The pointer can be positioned on an icon – a small picture indicating an option available with the aid of a mouse – and when the mouse is 'clicked', by pressing the left of two buttons the selected action is activated.

As is the case with all Windows software, the Lotus package has been particularly developed for you to make full use of the mouse. In practice, the mouse will offer many shortcuts over entering commands via a keyboard.

1.11 Data storage on disk

It has already been mentioned that data can be stored on both hard and floppy disks. Such data, however, has to be organised in a way that can be understood by the user and the computer. Data will be collected and stored in files.

For now, it is simply good enough to know what kind of files data are organised into. There are three types of file that Lotus users need to know about:

1 Operating System files contain the software that the computer needs to instruct it how to work. These files will appear on the hard disk before the Lotus package is ever introduced.

2 Applications software files will be large in number and the process of placing such files on to the hard disk is called installing the application.

3 Data keyed in by the user will be placed in one of the application directories. For each spreadsheet, for example, there will be a file with its own name, chosen by the user.

Disks, both floppy and hard, have a root directory which acts as a starting-point from which subdirectories are created, and into which files are stored.

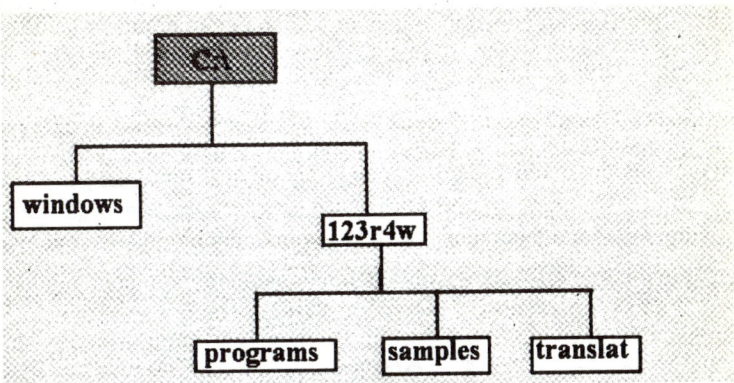

Table 1.1

In **Table 1.1** it can be seen that the root directory C: contains two subdirectories: windows and 123r4w. Lotus files are stored in the Lotus 123r4w subdirectory. However, you can move them to a further 'samples' directory if you wish. Organising files in directories is part of the process of file management. In many ways, it is no different to organising files in a filing cabinet. The art of good file management is one of knowing where to find information quickly and efficiently.

1.12 Computer memory

Computer memory is the memory which exists inside the computer other than on disk. Some computer memory is required to store programs needed to control the computer system – the Operating System. Much more memory is needed for two other main purposes:

1 To hold the application software when it is in use. Lotus 1-2-3 for Windows is a large software package made up of a great number of separate files all stored on hard disk. Not all of the package is loaded into memory at any one time; this is done only when it is needed. Lotus will frequently load files into memory to instruct it what to do in certain circumstances, and then dispose of this from memory when it is no longer required.

2 To hold data generated by the package itself. Again, not all data generated will need to be held in memory at any one time; it will be stored in many separate files and saved on disk.

The size of your computer memory (RAM – for Random Access Memory) is limited. Interacting with files stored on disk allows a computer to extend its capabilities considerably. It is important when buying software that you make sure your machine has enough memory in the computer itself to cope with the version of Lotus 1-2-3 for Windows you are buying. This is especially important when buying any package for Windows. Release 4 requires a minimum of 4 megabytes of RAM.

The more RAM your computer has, the better.

1.13 Menus

You will often come across the term "menu" when working with computers. A menu is simply a list of options that you can choose from. Quite often, when selecting a menu option you are given yet more options from that option – a sub-menu. This hierarchical structure of menus is now very common among applications on computers. In practice, the successful use of computer software often largely rests with the operator knowing his or her way around a set of menus.

A good deal of your effort in teaching yourself Lotus 1-2-3 for Windows will consist of finding your way around the Lotus menu structure. Lotus also has a large collection of SmartIcons that are used to bypass the menu structure and can be used to speed up many activities. The main emphasis throughout this book, however, is to become as familiar as possible with the menu structure of Lotus 1-2-3 for Windows.

1.14 Installing Lotus 1-2-3 for windows

When your software arrives you will receive:

- A number of floppy disks containing your software
- A reference manual

- A tutorial manual
- A set of instruction manuals one of which is an instruction book on setting up Lotus 1-2-3 for Windows on to your computer.

If your hard disk has been prepared in the correct way then the whole process of installing Lotus on to a hard disk has been made a little easier by Lotus, as they supply an installation program on one of the floppy disks. What the installation program will achieve is to place the required files on to your hard disk in the correct directories. It will also create the program icon in Program Manager, part of the Windows screen, giving you easy access to the program.

Assuming you have a hard disk system or are using a network, then to install the software all you need to do is:

- Switch your computer on and make sure Windows is running.
- Place the disk marked **installation** into your floppy disk drive. If you have two drives, then it should go into the one your system refers to as A : drive.
- Load up Windows if it is not running and, using your mouse, select the File option from the Program Manager menu. From here select 'Run' and enter the program name to run as A : INSTALL.

A set of instructions will appear on the menu guiding you through the installation procedures. When a package like Lotus 1-2-3 for Windows is purchased it is done on the understanding that it is for the use of the company or person who purchased it, and you will be required to enter the details of such a company. This forms part of the opening screen details when the package is loaded.

The rest of the installation procedure will require you simply to state where you want your spreadsheet software stored. As this package is a Windows based application, it will know a good deal about your system by the way the Windows software has been set up. For example, it will know what printers are on the system and what they are.

Follow the instructions as they appear; they are largely self-explanatory. You will need to have all the other disks at hand. Eventually you will leave the installation program and will find yourself back at the original window with the new Lotus 1-2-3 for Windows icon appearing and all ready for you to run.

If you have installed the software incorrectly, then you can always re-install it. To do this you can run the install program again in exactly the same way as you did before. If you re-run install or wish to make alterations to the way you installed the package in the first instance, you may not need to use all the disks again.

1.15 Getting started

With the diversity of operating systems and the different versions of Lotus 1-2-3, it is very difficult to give precise instructions about installing the package in a book like this. However, once installed, the rest is a little more straightforward.

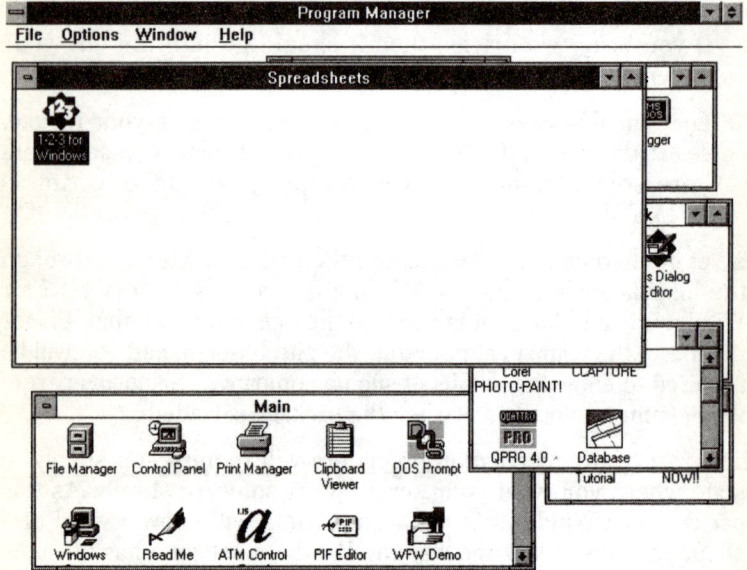

Screen dump 1.2

To get into Lotus 1-2-3 for Windows simply point the cursor at the icon with your mouse and perform a double click with the mouse to activate the program. **Screen dump 1.2** shows an example of a Windows screen from which you can select Lotus 1-2-3 for Windows. There will be a delay when you activate the loading of the spreadsheet. After this short delay you will be placed straight into the spreadsheet and ready to start. The empty spreadsheet you start with will look something like the one in **Screen dump 1.1**.

If you are working on a network system then the whole approach to loading Lotus 1-2-3 for Windows may be very different in that an opening screen may appear from which you select the Lotus package. Before progressing to the next chapter you are strongly advised to familiarise yourself with how to enter your particular set up of Lotus 1-2-3 for Windows, as variations on how to get started can be quite considerable.

1.16 Chapter summary

In this chapter you have covered the following points:

- what a spreadsheet is and what it can do;
- what software is and what hardware is needed to run Lotus 1-2-3 for Windows;
- the way data are stored in files and how directories are used to store files;
- how a hierarchical directory structure can be used to manage the file storage on a disk;
- how to install Lotus 1-2-3 for Windows on to a hard disk and subsequently how to get started with the Lotus package.

2
THE BASICS OF SPREADSHEETS

2.1 Aims of this chapter

The aim of this chapter is to help you get some idea of what a spreadsheet does and its style of operation. Most activities will be illustrated by examples as a way of investigating the capabilities of the Lotus package.

To begin with, it is assumed that you have installed your version of Lotus 1-2-3 for Windows on to your machine. If you have not done so, then refer to the sections in Chapter 1 on Installing Lotus 1-2-3 for Windows.

2.2 Getting started

- Switch on your machine and wait for either a DOS prompt or for Windows to load.
- If Windows has not automatically loaded, then load Windows now by typing WIN and pressing the enter key. Lotus 1-2-3 for Windows will only load and run within Microsoft Windows.
- Highlight the Lotus 1-2-3 icon with your mouse and double click the left button of the mouse.
- Once into the package you should see the blank spreadsheet illustrated in **Screen dump 2.1** with cell location A1 highlighted.

THE BASICS OF SPREADSHEETS

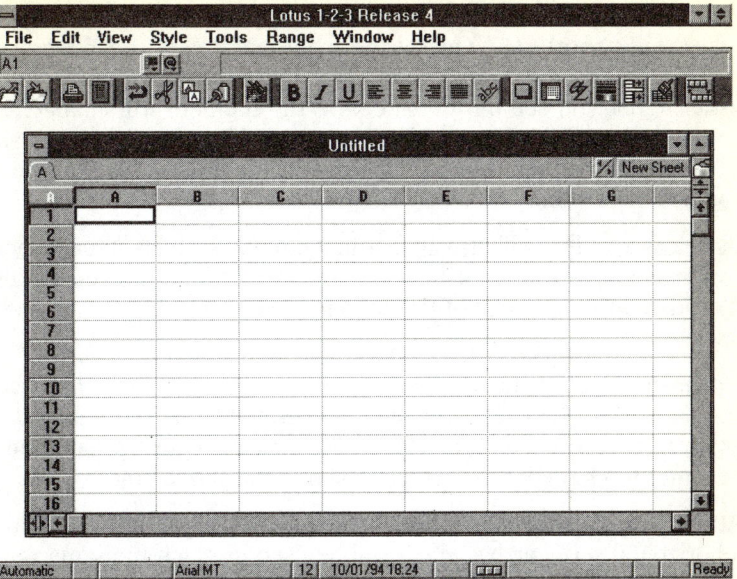

Screen dump 2.1

The control panel

The top five lines form the control panel. The first line contains the title and reads Lotus 1-2-3 Release 4 – [Untitled]. On the right are two square boxes containing the minimise and maximise buttons: ▼ ♦ to reduce the screen to an icon, and to fill the screen, respectively.

The second line is the menu bar:

File Edit View Style Tools Range Window Help

This menu will allow you to perform a whole host of actions with your spreadsheet which you will work with through this book. To the right of this bar appears a square control button ♦ which can be used to put the Release 4 sheet in a window. It is worth experimenting with this as it can be used to get the same appearance that is illustrated in the screen dumps.

The third line is called the Edit bar and at this stage is largely clear. The edit line will guide you when entering data and formulae in to your spreadsheet.

— 19 —

The fourth line shows a row of SmartIcons which are used to make time-saving short cuts. One of the main features of the Windows version of Lotus 1-2-3 is the comprehensive collection of such icons. What you see on the screen at the moment will change as you activate different parts of the package. Moreover, they are all customizable so that you can display icons that relate to actions that you use most often.

In Release 4 a line will also appear that indicates which spreadsheet you are using – the worksheet tab. At present it shows you are in spreadsheet A. The rest of the screen will contain the spreadsheet itself.

Down the right of the worksheet work area is a bar that has two splitter boxes ⬍. These will be demonstrated later. There is also a vertical scroll bar which will be used when your spreadsheet becomes too large for the screen to show it all at one time.

At the bottom of the worksheet work area appears another bar with a horizontal scroll arrow which will be used in much the same way as the vertical scroll to see parts of the spreadsheet that may not be visible on the screen.

At the very bottom of your screen appears a status line showing **Automatic** (which will be explained later); the default font **Arial**; the default font size **12**; date and time; a row of three buttons that will change the SmartIcons displayed; and the **Read**.

2.3 Columns and rows

The letters: A B C D E F G H that appear across the top of the worksheet below the control panel dictate the columns; the numbers 1–20 down the left-hand side indicate the rows. The highlighted part of the screen is situated at location Column A Row 1, referred to as cell A1.

You can navigate (move) from cell to cell by moving the pointer with the mouse and clicking the left-hand button to highlight the cell, or you can move from cell to cell with the arrow keys on the keyboards.

● Press the ⬇ key twice and the ➡ key once.

This should leave the cell pointer at cell **B3**. Look at the fourth line of the control panel to confirm this as being **A:B3**. The cell should be highlighted with a box surrounding it.

● Press your **Home** key to return to Cell **A1**.

Because there are in total 256 columns (lettered A . . . Z, AA, AB . . . BA, BB and up to IV) and 8,192 rows (numbered 1 . . . 8192), the entire spreadsheet is too large to fit on to your screen. **Screen dump 2.2** shows the far extremes of the spreadsheet. However, it is easy to move to any part of the spreadsheet without having to press the arrow keys, as the next section will show.

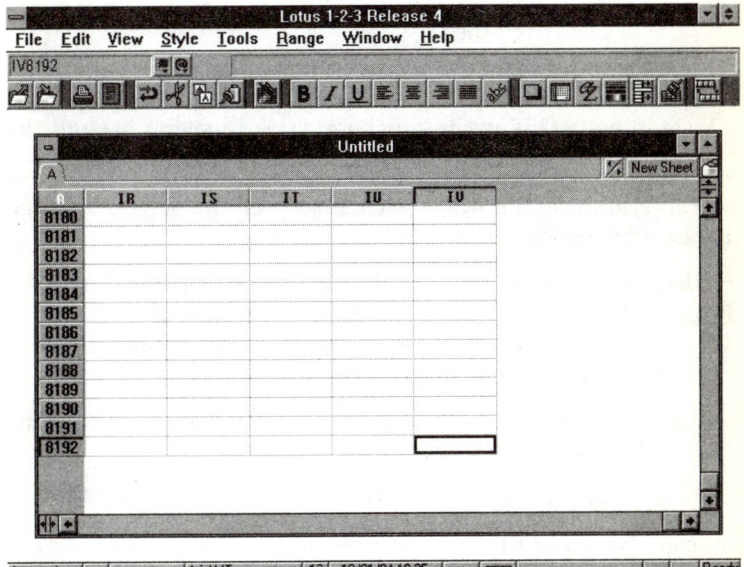

Screen dump 2.2

The rectangular box that highlights the position of the current cell will be referred to as the **cell pointer**.

2.4 Moving around the spreadsheet

The pointer can be moved around the spreadsheet from cell to cell with cursor control keys as shown. First, you can request a cell location by pressing function key **F5**, typing the cell location you want to move to, and pressing the **Enter** key.

- Press function key **F5**, type T100, and then press the **Enter** key.

As you did this, you will have observed that a **Go To** dialogue box appeared on your screen. Such dialogue boxes are a main feature of Lotus 1-2-3 for Windows.

You will now find yourself looking at a part of the spreadsheet quite distant from cell A1.

- Press the **Home** key on your keyboard to return to Cell A1, sometimes referred to as the Home position.
- Point the mouse arrow at a cell visible on your screen and press the left mouse button. The **cell pointer** will then highlight the located cell. This is the quickest way of moving around the screen.

You can also move the whole section seen on the screen by using another set of keys:

PgDn or **Page Down**	Moves one screen down
PgUp or **Page Up**	Moves one screen up
Tab	Moves one screen to the right
Shift & Tab (simultaneously)	Moves one screen to the left

- Use the keys listed above to get yourself familiar with navigating around the spreadsheet.
- Press the **Home** key on your keyboard to return to Cell A1.

You can also go to the far extremes of the working area of your spreadsheet using your mouse. On the right of the worksheet area you have a scroll box which is a small blank box. Position your mouse pointer on this box and, keeping the mouse key depressed, drag the box down to the end of the bar and let go. You should now be at the end of your spreadsheet. Exactly the same can be done with the bottom bar of your worksheet work area, allowing you to move to the far right of your spreadsheet. Without any data on the spreadsheet at present, it will not be possible to appreciate fully some of the facilities.

- Experiment with the scroll boxes as this will assist you well in future work.

The small scroll arrows by these boxes will also allow you to move the spreadsheet around your screen. However, this is better demonstrated when you have some data in your spreadsheet.

Moving the cell pointer off the end of the displayed spreadsheet either vertically or horizontally is known as scrolling. As you scroll, so new columns or row labels will appear and others will disappear. However, you will always be able to get back to them; information out of sight is not lost.

Another key to help you get around your spreadsheet, particularly if you do not have a mouse, is the **End** key. If you press the **End** key followed by the **Down Arrow** key you will go down to the end of the spreadsheet. If you press the **End** key followed by the **Right Arrow** key you will go to the far right of the spreadsheet.

2.5 Entering text

To begin with you can enter one of four types of data into a cell:

1 **A Number**. This is data of numeric value which can be used in calculations. You will see later in the book that other data, for example, percentage signs, can also be typed in.

2 **A Label**. This is essentially text such as names, addresses and sentences. Such text can contain numbers, or any type of character that appears on your keyboard. To enter a label, you have to have as the first character one of the following:

    a letter of the alphabet
- ' (apostrophe)
- " (double quote)
- ^ (claret – normally Shift + 6)
- \ (back slash)

Each of these prefixed characters has a different effect on how the text appears in the cell, which you will discover in due course, along with some others.

3 **A Formula**. This allows the calculation of figures based on what else appears in cells in other parts of the spreadsheet. To enter a formula, you will need to have as the first character either + (plus sign) or = (equals) or to enclose the formula between rounded brackets.

4 A Function. This is a built-in formula for mathematical, statistical, financial and other work. It begins with an **@** sign, and an example of such a function is: @SUM(B3 . . D5), which would sum up all numeric values bounded by the area of cells in the range from B3 to D5.

At this point you should be faced with an empty spreadsheet and should position the cell pointer in cell A1. Any entry you type will first be shown in the third line from the top of the screen. Now proceed with the instructions as follows, keeping an eye on what is happening on your screen.

- Type MY FIRST DEMONSTRATION. Note that a large cross and tick appear in the third line, next to the words you have typed. Press the **Enter** key.

- Press the **Down Arrow** key twice, type PRICE and then again press the **Down Arrow** key. Note how this last action entered the text *and* moved down to the next cell.

- Type COST and press the **Down Arrow** key.

- Type PROFIT and press the **Right Arrow** key. At this point the cursor should be in cell B5.

You will notice that what actually appears in the control panel is 'PROFIT not PROFIT. The apostrophe that prefixes the label is an indication that it is a label being entered rather than a number or formula.

Such entries of text into cells are referred to as labels. You will no doubt have noticed that these labels always appear in the far left-hand side of the cell, known as left justified. **Screen dump 2.3** shows what you should have at this stage. Later you will use other symbols to prefix labels, which will have a different effect.

If your text is not in upper case (capitals), do not worry at this stage, as it will not affect what you do for the rest of the demonstration.

You should be able to see on the screen that the label MY FIRST DEMONSTRATION has been written across adjacent cells. This is permissible only because no entries have been made into in these adjacent cells.

THE BASICS OF SPREADSHEETS

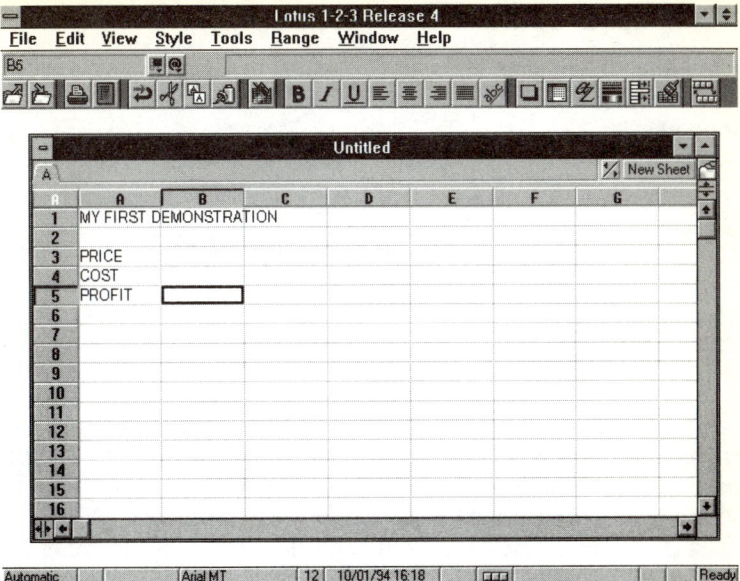

Screen dump 2.3

2.6 Correcting errors

However careful you are, mistakes are going to be made. There are two basic ways of correcting a cell entry. Suppose that the entry MY FIRST DEMONSTRATION was meant to read MY FIRST LOTUS DEMONSTRATION. To alter it you can select cell A1 by positioning the mouse pointer at cell A1 and clicking your left mouse button and then simply typing the correct label in as though the cell was empty. This will replace the old text with the new entry. Alternatively, you can use a function key to edit the cell contents.

● Position the cell pointer at cell A1 and press the function key **F2**.

● Use the **Left Arrow** key to move back along the text until you are positioned at the start of DEMONSTRATION. An alternative way would be to position the mouse arrow in front of DEMONSTRATION and clicking the left button (clicking on the space between FIRST and DEMONSTRATION).

— 25 —

- Now type LOTUS and press the **Enter** key.

When the text appears in the control panel in this way, you can use other editing keys such as the **Right Arrow** key and the **Back space** keys.

2.7 Entering numbers

Lotus distinguishes between *values* and *labels* simply through the first character. If the first character is a number (0–9) then a value is assumed, but if the first character is alphabetic, then a label is assumed. Hence, if you type: Over 18 years of age, Lotus 1-2-3 assumes this to be a label. If, however, you were to type: 18 and over, Lotus 1-2-3 Release 1 would register an input error as it would not be able to understand what it believes is a number (Release 4 has a facility of 'smart labels' which would detect this kind of entry as a label). To get Lotus 1-2-3 to accept such a string of characters that begins with a numeric character, you must include a ' (apostrophe) as the first character.

- Now type numbers into each of the cells B3 and B4. To do this, simply place the cell pointer into each cell and type, in turn, the number 69 in cell B3 and 60 in cell B4. On each occasion you must press the **Enter** key, or move the highlighted cell using the arrow keys.

Such numeric entries will be referred to as *values*.

2.8 Entering a formula

- Position the cell pointer in cell B5 and type +B3–B4 and press the **Enter** key. You have now entered a formula. (Note that this could also have been entered as = B3–B4).

The calculation of cell B3 minus cell B4 (69–60) now appears in cell B5. The input line of the control panel shows the formula; the cell shows the result. This demonstrates how the appearance on the spreadsheet alone will not reveal what is actually in the cells.

Lotus 1-2-3 has distinguished your entry in cell B5 as a formula by the fact that it starts with + or = (or is in brackets) and refers to other cell locations. As a technical point, it is worth noting that cell references in formulae are not case sensitive; in other words, (b3–b4) reads exactly the same as (B3–B4).

At this stage you will have a spreadsheet with Labels in cells A1, A3, A4 and A5, values in cells B3 and B4, and a formula in cell B5. On a very small scale this is what spreadsheets are all about. Try altering the price and cost cell, preferably moving from cell to cell with the aid of your mouse to position the cell pointer. Before going any further, experiment by creating more cell entries with extra formulae. For example, add a new cell that shows the profit percentage over selling price. +B5/B3*100.

A summary of the special characters to use in formulae would now be useful:

 + Add
 – Subtract
 * Multiply
 / Divide
 (Open bracket (rounded bracket only)
) Close bracket (rounded bracket only)

Building up a formula in Lotus 1-2-3 conforms to all the normal rules of mathematical formulae.

2.9 Saving your work

In order to save your spreadsheet you will need to select the save option from the menu at the top of the screen.

- Select the option by positioning the mouse pointer over the menu bar option File and pressing the left mouse button to see the sub-menu 'pulled down' over that part of the screen.

Such menus are called 'pull-down menus' because you appear to pull the menus down from the top of the screen.

- As an alternative to using the mouse you can select the menu by holding down the **Alt** key and pressing the character key that is underlined in the menu option required, in this case F. Holding down the **Alt** key and pressing the F key will produce the pull-down menu that you produced using the mouse.

Screen dump 2.4 shows the menu that you will see on your screen. The option you want is 'Save As'. This allows you to save your work in a file with a name of your choice. The other options will be explained later in the book.

- With this menu displayed select Save As either by clicking on the option with your mouse or by pressing the **Down Arrow** key or by pressing the **A** key (the underlined character in the option Save As).

- Now enter a filename. Give it the name FIRSTGO by typing this in and then pressing the **Enter** key.

If, at a later stage, you wish to save changes you make to the file you can use the Save option rather than Save As. This will save the modified spreadsheet using the same file name.

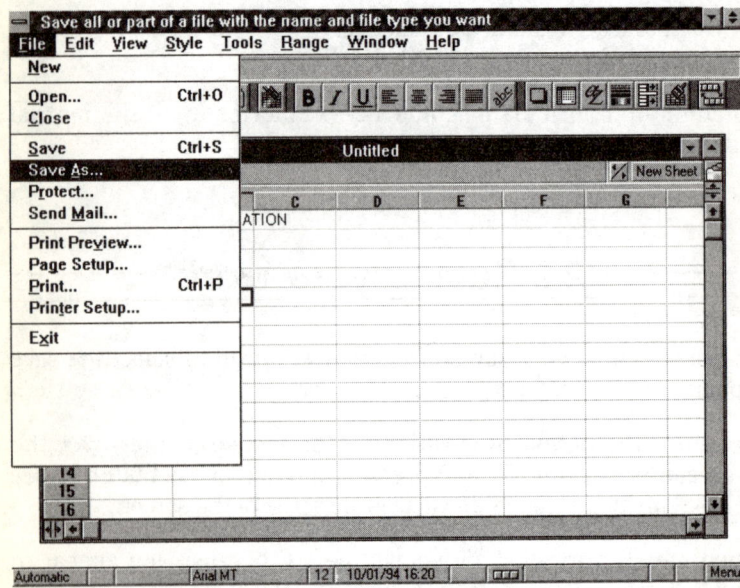

Screen dump 2.4

When you save your work, Lotus 1-2-3 automatically gives the file an extension name: .WK4 (WK3 for Release 1). It has also saved the file in a directory for you.

An alternative to using the menu command would be to click on the second SmartIcon from the left.

2.10 Printing your work

To complete the process, you can print the spreadsheet. (If you do not have a printer installed then skip this section.)

- Click on the File option from the menu bar. Then select the Print option from the pull-down menu.

- Alternatively, if you prefer not to use the mouse, then select the commands by holding down the **Alt** key and pressing F followed by P for Print.

In time the various print options will be explained. For now you will use the shortest and easiest way.

Screen dump 2.5 illustrates the panel that appears. The boxes that need completing require details about pages to be printed and the Range to be printed.

Selecting what you want printed is determining what part of the spreadsheet to print. Lotus defines 'chunks' or blocks of the spreadsheet as RANGES. Hence, what you need to do is to define the range to be printed. For this purpose, the mouse will be very useful.

Lotus 1-2-3 for Windows will try to 'guess' about what you want printed. At this stage, it assumes you want the current spreadsheet printed, as opposed to a range or a collection of worksheets.

The panel that appears on your screen is there to allow you to make any alterations to these settings.

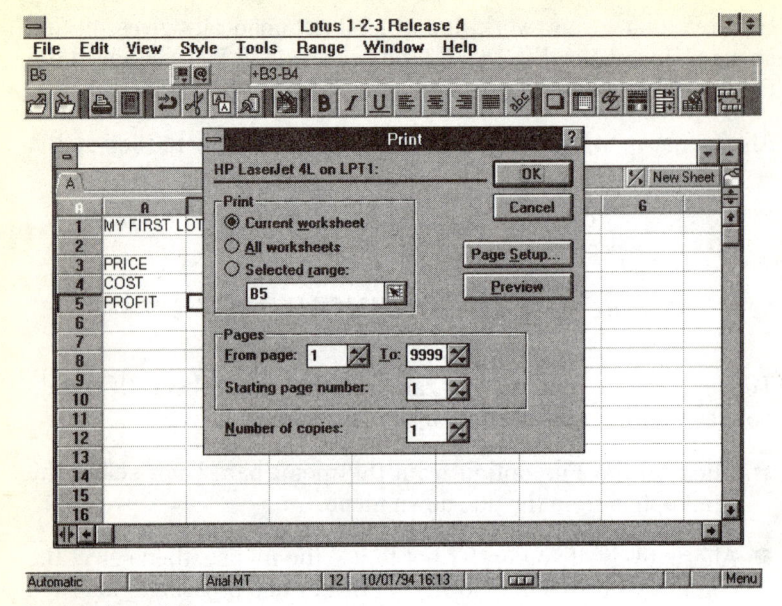

Screen dump 2.5

- Click on B5 in the Print box. It will change colour. Now type A1 .. B5 and then press the **Enter** key.

What this does is to define the range as being the rectangular block of cells that have A1 and B5 at the corners.

- Now click on the OK button.

This should activate the printer and a print-out of your work should appear. Meanwhile, on screen you will return to the spreadsheet. If an error has occurred, then it is probably because your printer was not on-line or the computer does not have a printer installed. You can still work with Lotus 1-2-3, but you will not be able to print out your work.

If no error message has appeared and your printer is not printing, then it may be because the output has been stored in a file for later printing from the Print Manager program within Windows. If this is the case, then you will have to activate this programme to print. Refer to your Windows manual or *Teach Yourself Windows* for help.

Printing from the spreadsheet can be done more quickly by using the mouse:

THE BASICS OF SPREADSHEETS

- Return to the spreadsheet by leaving the menu. This should be the state you are at when you have finished printing. If not, press the **Esc** key on your keyboard.

- Click on cell A1 and, **keeping the left mouse button depressed** move the pointer to the right and downwards. The area changes colour. When you take your finger off the mouse button the area remains in this different colour and has now become **highlighted**. Highlight the block of 10 squares, as in **Screen dump 2.6**.

- With the mouse, select the third icon from the left of the row of Smart Icons. This is the printer icon.

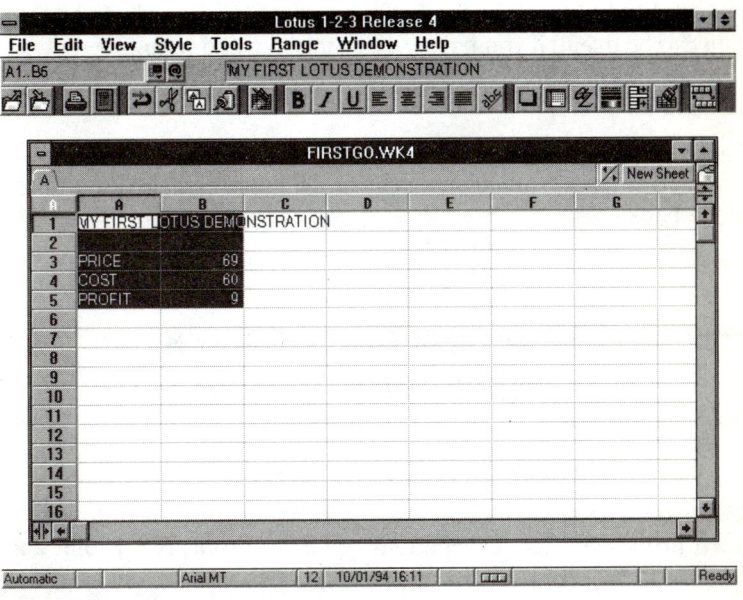

Screen dump 2.6

This will give you the print dialogue box requiring you to select **OK** to start printing. The result should be to print this highlighted range.

2.11 Erasing data from a spreadsheet

To produce a more sophisticated spreadsheet, erase the existing data.

- Move the cell pointer to A1 (the Home position).
- Highlight the range, with your mouse, A1 through to B5.
- Select from the menu bar the Edit pull-down menu.
- From the pull-down menu, select the option Clear. Click the OK button in the clear dialogue box.

The highlighted area will have cleared. This method of clearing data can be useful if you have made a mistake and wish to re-enter a number of cell entries. Always save the spreadsheet first before deleting anything.

There are other ways of deleting ranges of data, such as deleting specified rows or columns, which will be explained at a later stage in the book.

2.12 A new spreadsheet – sales performance

It is now time to produce a more sophisticated spreadsheet.

The text and data will have to be typed in as you would do with a word processor. The calculations of Gross Profit, Net Profit, and totals are made by Lotus 1-2-3.

- Click on cell C3 and type the quarter-yearly heading Jan-Mar. Using the **Right Arrow** move to cell D3 and type Apr-Jun. Continue with Jul-Sep in cell E3, Oct-Dec in cell F3, and YEAR in cell G3.

If you want to enter text into a cell and centre it within that cell rather then leave it left-justified, then you should prefix the text typed with the ^ sign rather than just typing it into the cell. This method of centring text should not be done with the numbers, as

THE BASICS OF SPREADSHEETS

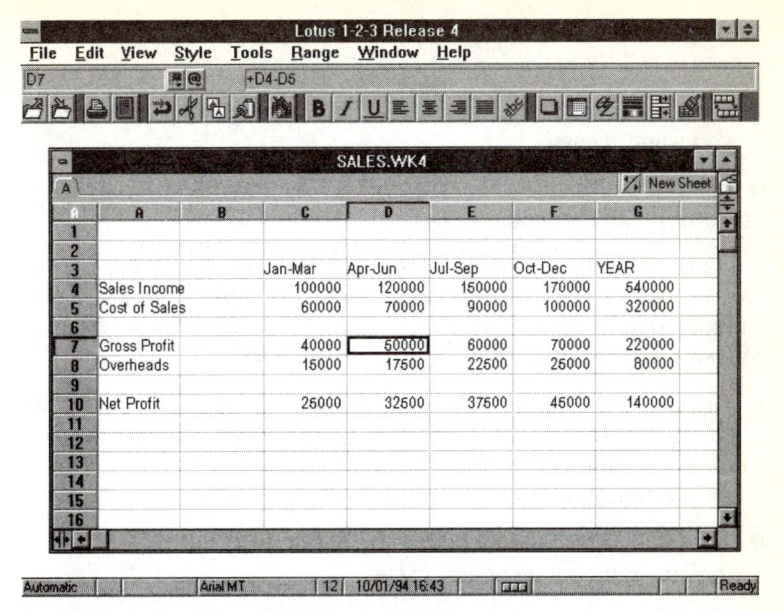

Screen dump 2.7

Lotus 1-2-3 will not recognise the cell entry as a number and so cannot use it for calculations.

- Now type the other labels required: Sales Income in cell A4, Cost of Sales in A5, Gross Profit in cell A7, Overheads in cell A8 and Net Profit in cell A10.

- Now type the data for Sales Income and Cost of Sales for each of the four quarters (8 numbers in total).

All the remaining figures will be calculated by Lotus 1-2-3 using formulae that you will type in.

- Click on cell C7 and type the formula +C4–C5. When you press the **Enter** key the correct figure for Gross Profit should appear, i.e. Sales Income less Cost of Sales.

Instead of entering the formulae for the remaining quarters, you will use a different technique.

- Click on G5, type @SUM(C5 .. F5) and press the **Enter** key. This adds up all the Cost of Sales figures.

- In cell G4 type a function for adding up the Sales Income figures: @SUM(C4 .. F4).

Now you will use the copying facility to copy the formulae that appear in cell C7 to appear in the cells D7 to G7.

- Click on cell C7 because this is the cell containing the formula you want to copy.

- Select from the menu bar the option **E**dit and then from the pull-down menu the option **C**opy.

Although nothing appears to have happened, Lotus 1-2-3 has placed the cell contents into the system Clipboard. This is a part of the memory that is used to store data on a temporary basis. What is needed now is to paste this into the spreadsheet.

- Highlight the range D7 to G7 using your mouse. To achieve this, click the mouse pointer at cell D7 and, holding the left mouse button down, drag the pointer to cell G7 and the let the mouse button go.

- Now select from the menu bar the option **E**dit and then from the pull-down menu the option **P**aste.

It should now be apparent that the method and principle of highlighting a range of cells is useful and well worth learning as it can be used to save a considerable amount of keyboard work.

The next stage is to type in a formula for the Overhead figures. For this purpose it has been assumed that Overheads are to be 25% of Cost of Sales. Given this assumption, proceed as follows:

- Click on cell C8 and type the formula +C5*25%. Note how 25% is recorded as 0.25 in the formula in the third line of the control panel. Note also that the correct figure: 15,000 appears in the cell.

Do not use the copy command just yet because there is an even better way of saving time. Net Profit is Gross Profit less Overheads.

- Click on cell C10, type the formula +C8−C9, and press the **Enter** key.

The next stage will be to copy both the Overheads formula and the Net Profit formula for the other quarters and for the year in a single action:

- Highlight the range of cells C8 to C10.

- Now select from the menu bar the option **E**dit and then from the pull-down menu the option **C**opy.

- Highlight the range of cells D8 to G10. This will define a range of three rows and four columns.

- Select from the menu bar the option Edit and then Paste.

This has enabled you to copy two sets of formulae in a single operation. What you have now done is fundamental to making spreadsheet handling quick and easy to set up. If you are unclear at this stage about what has happened, then give yourself time to experiment.

This now completes the spreadsheet. At this stage you should experiment by changing some of the numbers (not the formulae). If you change some of the quarterly Sales Income figures, or Cost of Sales figures, the rest of the spreadsheet will adjust by recalculating Gross Profit, Overheads, Net Profits and Year totals.

Now print and save the spreadsheet as you did in the previous section of this chapter, remembering the sequence of events:

- Highlight what you want printed; click on the Print SmartIcon; click OK.

- Save your spreadsheet by selecting from the menu bar the option File, then Save As, typing SALES, and clicking **OK**.

If you have not been able to follow all of this or feel unable to remember how everything was achieved, do not worry. You will get further help and practice as you work through the book.

You will now have performed the typical process involved in producing a spreadsheet, namely:

1 Opening Lotus 1-2-3 for Windows.

2 Prepare a spreadsheet with Labels, Values and Formulae.

3 Enter a varied number of values to see what the results would be.

4 Save the spreadsheet in a file with a filename.

5 Highlight the range in the spreadsheet.

6 Print the highlighted spreadsheet.

2.13 Asking for help

At any time while working through a spreadsheet, Lotus 1-2-3 offers you various levels of help. You can get help by pressing function key **F1**. Doing this produces a screen similar to the one in **Screen dump 2.8**.

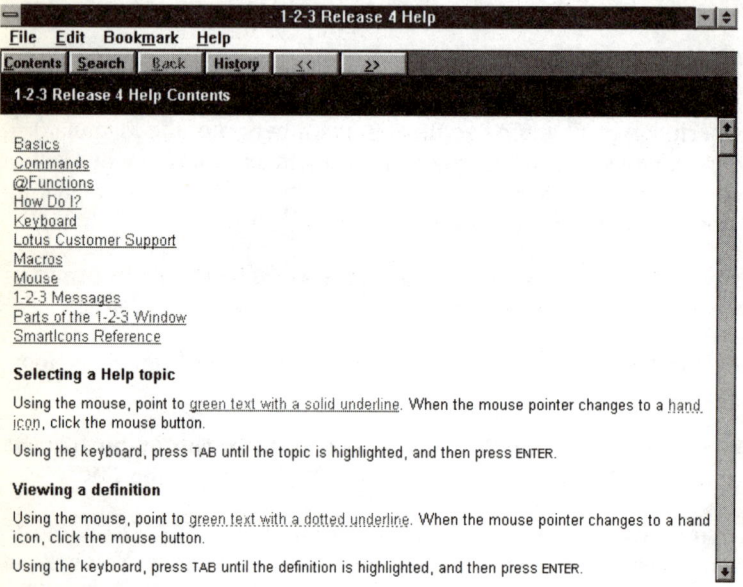

```
┌─────────────────────────────────────────────────────────────┐
│                    1-2-3 Release 4 Help                     │
│ File  Edit  Bookmark  Help                                  │
│ Contents │ Search │ Back │ History │ << │ >>                │
│ 1-2-3 Release 4 Help Contents                               │
│                                                             │
│ Basics                                                      │
│ Commands                                                    │
│ @Functions                                                  │
│ How Do I?                                                   │
│ Keyboard                                                    │
│ Lotus Customer Support                                      │
│ Macros                                                      │
│ Mouse                                                       │
│ 1-2-3 Messages                                              │
│ Parts of the 1-2-3 Window                                   │
│ SmartIcons Reference                                        │
│                                                             │
│ Selecting a Help topic                                      │
│ Using the mouse, point to green text with a solid underline.│
│ When the mouse pointer changes to a hand icon, click the    │
│ mouse button.                                               │
│ Using the keyboard, press TAB until the topic is            │
│ highlighted, and then press ENTER.                          │
│                                                             │
│ Viewing a definition                                        │
│ Using the mouse, point to green text with a dotted          │
│ underline. When the mouse pointer changes to a hand         │
│ icon, click the mouse button.                               │
│ Using the keyboard, press TAB until the definition is       │
│ highlighted, and then press ENTER.                          │
└─────────────────────────────────────────────────────────────┘
```

Screen dump 2.8

This screen gives you the contents list of some of the help topics available within Lotus 1-2-3. As you move the mouse pointer through the list: Basics, Commands, @Functions, a small hand will appear. When you click on a topic a new page appears. To scroll through the list click on the scroll boxes on the right side of the screen.

You could spend a considerable amount of time looking through the many pages of help available. Pressing the **Esc** key on your keyboard will return you to your spreadsheet at the same position and state you left it.

As mentioned, Lotus 1-2-3 has different levels of help. To see what this means:

THE BASICS OF SPREADSHEETS

- Click on the File option from the menu bar.
- Press function key **F1**.

Now you get a help screen that tells you what the facilities are in the File pull-down menu.

- Press the **Esc** key to return to the spreadsheet.

Finally, click on the save SmartIcon to save your most recent changes. Then click on the File option from the menu bar, and select Exit from the pull-down menu. You will quit Lotus 1-2-3 and return to the Windows screen.

In this chapter you have created two spreadsheets which have been saved on your disk and which can be retrieved at a later stage.

2.14 Chapter summary

You have covered the following points:

- How to load Lotus 1-2-3.
- To identify the control panel, the menu bar and the SmartIcons at the top of the screen.
- To move around or navigate the spreadsheet in a variety of different ways.
- To highlight cells.
- To distinguish different types of cell entries: labels, numbers, formulae, and functions.
- To correct typing errors.
- To use the menu bar and the pull-down menus.
- To define and highlight ranges.
- To use options from the Edit pull-down menu to copy and to erase ranges of cells.
- To print spreadsheets.
- To use File commands to Save, Save As, and Exit.
- To use SmartIcons to save a file and to print a range.
- To use the Help pages.

3
MENUS, PRINTING AND FILING

3.1 Aims of this chapter

One of the principal features of getting to know any software package is being able to find your way around the menu system. Lotus 1-2-3 is no exception to this. It has a hierarchical structure of menus which you have already encountered. The first level appears across the menu bar near the top of your screen with the next level pulled down when you implement it. Further levels are then available produced as you implement further options. This chapter will make you more familiar with the menu structure and help you understand the main options you will commonly need when using the spreadsheet. With many of the menu options, a dialogue box will appear rather than another pull-down menu.

In describing the menu system, emphasis has been placed on saving and retrieving files to and from your hard disk as well as being able to print your spreadsheet. Although these were all introduced in the previous chapter, this chapter investigates these facilities in much more detail.

Although the emphasis in this, and future chapters, will be on using the menu structure in order to help you get familiar with it, Lotus 1-2-3 also has a large collection of **SmartIcons** that by-pass the menu system and are designed to help you speed up operations. These will be illustrated alongside the menu system.

3.2 Changing the style of your spreadsheet

You have already been introduced to how to write and save a file. Reproduce the spreadsheet depicted in **Screen dump 3.1**. The spreadsheet contains no formulae or functions, just labels and numbers. You will notice that column A is not wide enough to hold the label Wednesday; leave it as it stands for now because you will learn how to widen the cell.

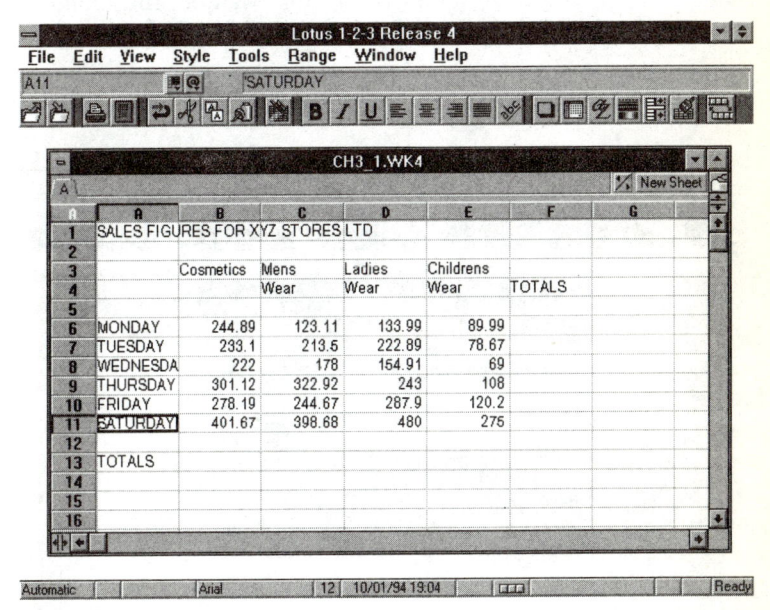

	A	B	C	D	E	F
1	SALES FIGURES FOR XYZ STORES LTD					
2						
3		Cosmetics	Mens	Ladies	Childrens	
4			Wear	Wear	Wear	TOTALS
5						
6	MONDAY	244.89	123.11	133.99	89.99	
7	TUESDAY	233.1	213.5	222.89	78.67	
8	WEDNESDA	222	178	154.91	69	
9	THURSDAY	301.12	322.92	243	108	
10	FRIDAY	278.19	244.67	287.9	120.2	
11	SATURDAY	401.67	398.68	480	275	
12						
13	TOTALS					

Screen dump 3.1

Before saving the file, you will use the menu structure to set all numbers in the spreadsheet to two decimal places and to widen column A.

The first step before saving the file will be to **FORMAT** all numbers to two decimal places. This involves altering the **STYLE** of the spreadsheet.

- Highlight the range of cells where the numbers are stored: B6 to E11. At this stage it is worth your discovering that this can be done via your keyboard. Holding down the **Shift** key, press the **Arrow** keys to move the cell pointer and highlight a block.

- Click on the Style option from the menu bar. Then select Number Format.

[If you are a Release 1 user, then the Number Format option is found in the Range pull-down menu.]

- In the dialogue box, click on **Fixed** in the **Format** box.

The **Format** box contains a list of available formats and the **Fixed** option is at the top of the list. The scroll bar to the right of the **Format** box allows you to scroll up and down this list with your mouse. When you have found the format wanted, the mouse is again used to highlight it by clicking the left mouse button.

At this stage, you should have **Screen dump 3.2**, which shows the **Number Format** dialogue box.

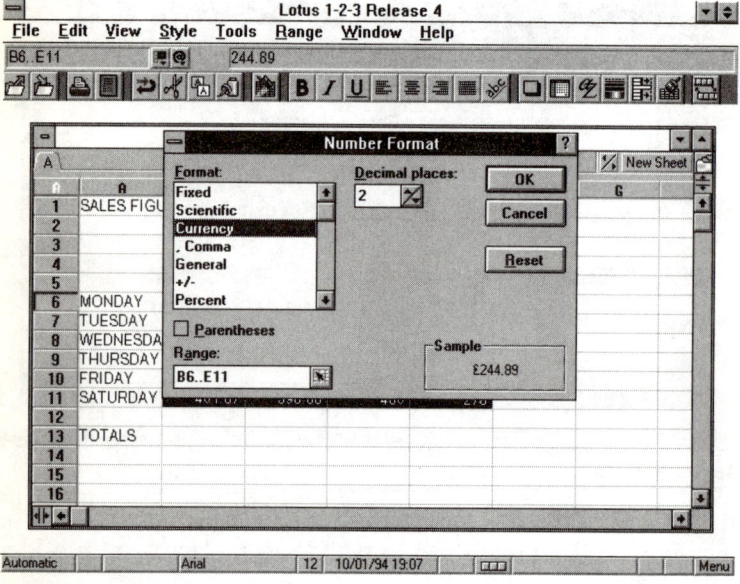

Screen dump 3.2

The rest of the settings are correct: the default of 2 decimal places and the range B6 .. E11.

- Click on the OK button, or press the **Enter** key.

All the numbers will have been expanded to 2 decimal places. Next you can widen column A so that the whole of the word Wednesday can be seen. Lotus starts off with all columns set to

9 characters wide. You will need to have column A at least 10 characters wide.

- Click on cell C8.
- Click on Style in the menu bar, then Column Width.

[If you are a Release 1 user, then the Column Width option is found in the Worksheet pull-down menu.]

- Click on the dot next to Fit widest entry and then click on the OK button. The column will expand to accommodate the word Wednesday.

Formatting numbers and sizing columns to fit the widest entries can be performed using SmartIcons, and these will be explained later.

3.3 The menu structure

This method of altering the appearance of the spreadsheet will be discussed again on many occasions and, in particular, later in this chapter. You should by now be getting a good appreciation of how the menu structure and their dialogue boxes work. In most cases, you will pull down a menu, select an option and then complete a dialogue box of settings (or parameters). Or you will simply click on a SmartIcon that you can position above, below, or on either side of the working area.

Remember when you use the menu bar you will notice that one character in each option is underlined. If you hold down the **Alt** key and then press the letter underlined, this will implement the pull-down menu.

When dialogue boxes appear, their options will also have a single character underlined. You can also use your keyboard to select these by holding down the **Alt** key and then pressing the appropriate letter.

While working with the menus there is always an important source of help available. You will see prompts given in the control panel at the top of your screen. These prompts will give you basic instructions as to what input is expected and are often enough to remind you about the detailed operation of many facilities.

Function key **F1** gives you help at any stage and is, in itself, a menu structure of help facilities. It is time well spent exploring the help structure as it is a means that will often solve awkward problems.

3.4 Saving a file

This next section explains in a little more detail the process of saving your file.

- Click on the File option from the menu bar. Then select the Save As option, and type the name STORE.

You will notice that there are many options available in the File pull-down menu. A little explanation is now in order.

New: This opens a new spreadsheet. When a new spreadsheet is started, an old one remains. You will experiment with this in a later chapter.

Open: This allows you to open a spreadsheet that already exists without loosing the one you are currently working with.

Close: This closes the current spreadsheet file. This option will prompt you for a file name if you have not saved the most current version.

Save: This will allow you to save a file that you have either saved before or one that you have retrieved. In other words, it saves the file under the same name previously given. If the spreadsheet has no name, you will be asked for a file name.

Save As: This will save an existing spreadsheet with another file name or will save a spreadsheet that has not previously been saved. You will always be prompted for a file name using this option.

The other options require a little more investigation before you can make full use of them. However, knowing what they can do will increase your understanding of basic concepts. [Some of the remaining options may differ according to the version of the package you have.]

Protect. This allows you to protect a file from being altered in certain ways. If you have spent time creating a spreadsheet that you want to use for reference later, then protecting it from unwanted alterations and deletion can be a useful safeguard. You can remove the protection at a later stage.

Send Mail. This allows you to send a spreadsheet, or parts of it, to other users and other applications. The use of this requires extra software in addition to the Lotus 1-2-3 spreadsheet. Consequently, this facility is not a topic for this book.

Print Preview. This allows you to see your file as it will appear when it is printed.

Page Setup. This lets you determine the way the spreadsheet will appear when printed. Lotus 1-2-3 will set the page layout for you, but this allows you to alter things like headers and footers, orientation, and margins.

Print. This prints your spreadsheet or a range of the spreadsheet that has been defined. It can also be used to print your graphs.

Printer Setup. This is used to set up your printer differently from the way it is set up by the Windows printer control.

Exit. Returns to the Windows screen.

At the foot of this menu may appear a list of files, if you are a Release 4 user. This allows you quickly to open a file. The list is generated from the most recent files you have used. As you work more with Lotus 1-2-3, you will see this list grow and change.

You will not need most of these options, but they are there to allow you to tailor the spreadsheet package more effectively to your particular needs.

- Having saved STORE.WK4, select the Close option from the File pull-down menu.

At this point you should have an empty spreadsheet.

Opening a file is the reverse of saving one.

- Click on File and select Open.

You will now see the Open File dialogue box. If your file does not appear in the Filename box, it may be because there is not enough room in the window to display all the available file names. Use the arrow keys to scroll through the file names. As an alternative to the arrow keys, you can use your mouse to move the box between the up and down arrows.

- Select the file saved as STORE by clicking on it with the mouse. Highlight the file name. Then click on the OK button.

The STORE.WK4 file should now reappear on your screen.

3.5 Expanding your spreadsheet

Now you can add to the spreadsheet. First, type in formulae for the totals in column F.

- Click on cell F6.
- Type the start of the function: @SUM(

Instead of typing in the range where the numbers are located, you can highlight the range in the same way as you have highlighted ranges before.

- Use either your arrow keys or mouse to position the cell pointer on cell B6.
- Now hold down the left mouse button and move the mouse pointer to E6 so that the range is highlighted. (Holding down the **Shift** key and pressing the **Arrow** keys can be used as an alternative to using the mouse.)
- Let go of the mouse button and press the **Enter** key. (Or let go of the **Shift** and **Arrow** keys if you are using your keyboard.)

The desired result should be to total the numbers in the columns. Check that this is so. The function cell F6 should be @SUM(B6 .. E6).

The next objective is to copy this formula to the range F7 .. F11.

- Position the cell pointer at cell F6 where the formula has been entered. This is the one you need to copy.
- Click on Edit and select Copy.

This has stored the formula in the Clipboard and would appear to have done nothing.

- Highlight the range of cells F7 to F11.

MENUS, PRINTING AND FILING

- Click on Edit and select Paste.

You now have daily totals for the complete store. Next you should type in formulae to add up the weekly totals for each department, and one for the overall sales of the store.

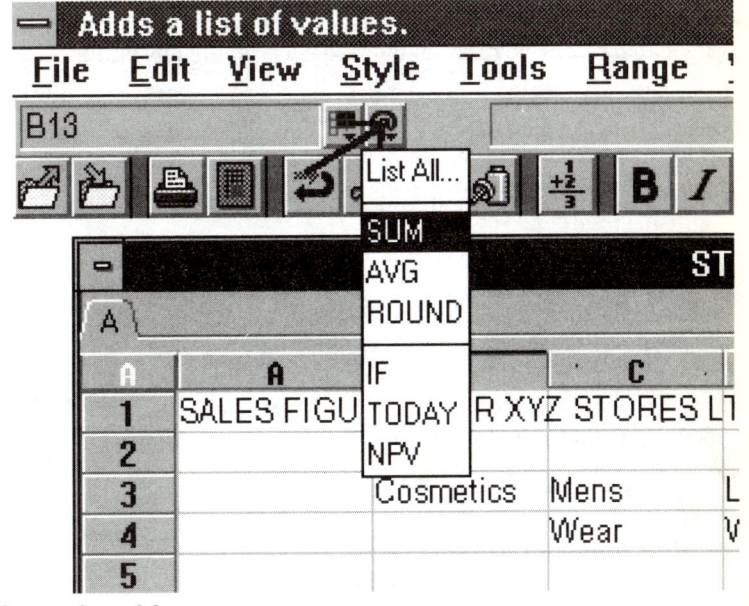

Screen dump 3.3

- Click on cell B13. Then click on the Formulae SmartIcon, then click on Sum from the pull-down menu, as shown in screen-dump 3.3.

- Highlight cells B6 to B11 and then click on the tick icon. The figure 1680.97 should appear in cell B13 and the formula @SUM(B6..B11) in the control panel. Copy the formula in cell B13 to the range C13 to F13.

- Type a label, right justified, in cell A13 as TOTALS. Remember, to right justify you need to prefix the label with ".

You will also notice at this stage that the format of the numbers determined by the formulae is not to two places of decimals. Moreover, the figures are not in £ sterling, so the next stage will be to format all numbers to two places of decimals as currency.

- Highlight the range of cells from B6 to F13.

- Click on the Style option from the menu bar.
- Select the Number Format option from the pull-down menu.

[If you are a Release 1 user then select the Format option from the Range pull-down menu instead.]

- Click on currency in the Format box. You will see that the Decimal places box is already 2, so click on the OK button.

If you are a Release 1 user the figures may well be quoted in dollars. To alter the currency symbol you will need to use another part of the menu system.

- Click on the Tools option from the menu bar.
- Select User Setup option from the pull-down menu.
- Click on the International option.

A dialogue box will appear with various settings. If the currency is as you require, then it can be left unaltered. Other settings can also be made at this stage, such as the format you want the date to appear at the bottom of your spreadsheet.

- Type in £ as a replacement for $.
- Click on the OK button when you are satisfied that the settings are correct.

[Later versions of Lotus 1-2-3 have the £ currency symbol as a default and so will need no alterations. To change for example, to dollars: Highlight the relevant cells. Click on the Tools option from the menu bar. Then select User Setup. Click on International in the dialogue Box, then type the $ symbol in the Symbol for currency line in the Currency box. Click on OK in the International box, then OK in the User Setup box.]

Next, you will remove the grid lines that appear on the spreadsheet.

- Click on the View option from the menu bar. Then select the Set View Preferences option.

[If you are Release 1 user the same facility is available in the Window menu as Display Options.]

The resulting dialogue box allows you to make considerable changes to the appearance of your spreadsheet.

- To remove the grid lines, click on the Grid lines box. When there is no cross in the box, the grid lines will not appear on the spreadsheet.

The spreadsheet should now look similar to that shown in **Screen dump 3.4**.

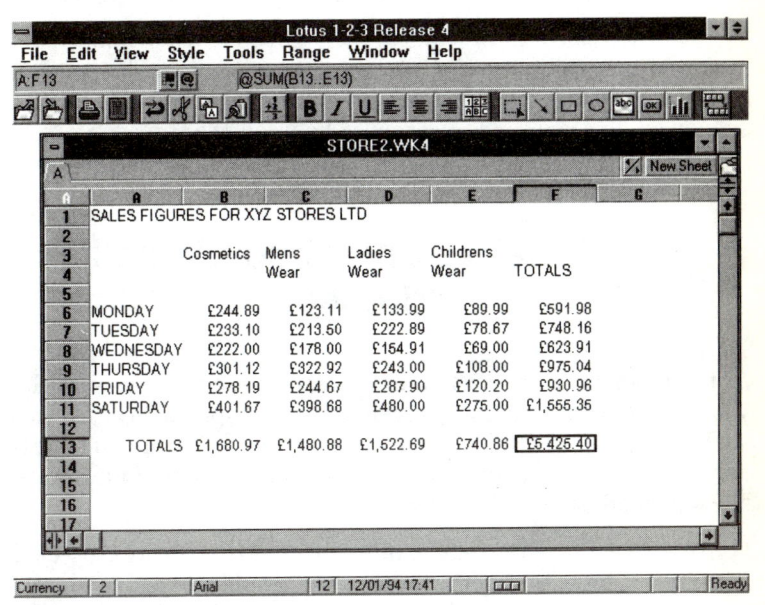

Screen dump 3.4

Before moving on to the next section, it is now a useful exercise to look again at what you had before making these additions.

The first stage will be to save your file under a different name:

- Click on the File option from the menu bar. Then select the Save As option.

- Save the file with the file name STORE2.

- Click on File option. Then select Open. From the list of files, select STORE again, and click the OK button to open the file.

You now have two copies of the same file. The last one you opened will be visible on your screen. This is the file you started with.

- Click on the Window option from the menu bar. [If there is a Pick option showing, then select it. Newer versions of Lotus do not require this.]

This now presents you with the files open to you to pick from. If you pick STORE2 then you will be returned to that sheet. (In an application of this kind, the store could, for instance, keep a spreadsheet for each week of the year. You could then open different weeks and make various comparisons.)

You can hop back and forth between spreadsheets making alterations to one without affecting the others. You can also work in either spreadsheet without affecting the other. Chapter 9 has a section on how you can link formulae between two spreadsheets.

3.6 Relative and absolute cell addresses

At the moment, keep both spreadsheets open and make sure that you have selected the most recently created spreadsheet to work with, namely, STORE2. This section will examine the more advanced features of copying formulae from one part of the spreadsheet to another.

On row 15 you will create a new formula that expresses each department total as a percentage of the grand Total. The departmental percentage is the departmental total divided by the overall total and expressed as a percentage. In this exercise, you will need to type in a formula in cell B15 to express this figure and then copy the formula across the other departments. The problem with this is that when you copy the formula the relative position of the overall total will alter for each department.

In a formula, a reference to a cell that does not change when you copy the formula is called an ABSOLUTE reference. An absolute reference always refers to the same cell or range. To create an absolute cell reference, type a $ (dollar sign) before the column letter and row number when you write the formula. Here, F13 becomes the absolute cell reference in the formula needed in cell B13.

- Highlight cell B15 and type in the formula +B13/$F$13

The result will appear as a decimal and will need to be formatted as a percentage. This will be done later.

MENUS, PRINTING AND FILING

- Now copy the cell B15 to the range C15 to E15.

As an exercise, repeat the two steps just undertaken but with the formula B13/F13 in cell B15. Try to see what has happened by looking at each formula through the range. Then go back to correct the formula.

Now you need to alter the format so that percentages are shown.

- Highlight the range of cells B15 to E15.
- Click on the Style option. Then select Number Format.
- Click on the Percent option in the Number Format dialogue box.
- Set the number of Decimal places to 0 (zero). Click on the OK button.

As a next task, you will introduce two new departments: Electrical and Furniture. These two new departments will appear between Cosmetics and Men's Wear. To do this, you will need to insert two new columns.

- Click on column letter C. The entire column is now highlighted.
- Click on the Edit option. Then select Insert.
- Repeat this to insert a second blank column.

The effect of this has been to insert two columns and shift the columns to the right two columns along. Release 4 users will note that the formulae in all cells have been preserved. [If you are a Release 1 user, then you will need to format the new cells.]

- Now type in the new headings for the Electrical and Furniture departments. Try the following, as these numbers will prove useful in the remaining parts of this chapter:

	Electrical	Furniture
Monday	322	0
Tuesday	291	1,200
Wednesday	228.23	100
Thursday	256.12	499.99
Friday	331.2	5,400
Saturday	410.1	12,099

If the new numbers entered do not have the format in the same way as the others you will need to format the new range for currency.

Now the end column is off the screen because the spreadsheet is too wide. As a further demonstration of the windows facilities, you will next create a vertical window in column B that allows you to move around the table of figures and be able to see the days of the week remain in the left most part of the screen.

- Click on column letter B. The entire column is now highlighted.

- Click on the View option [Window pull down menu if you are using Release 1]. Then select Split. Click on Vertical in the Type box in the dialogue box. Then click on the OK button.

You have now split your screen into two windows, with both windows showing the same spreadsheet, but at differing points. To move between windows you can either press function key **F6** or click the mouse on the window you want to work in. The advantage of having two versions of the same spreadsheet open is that you can keep the days of the week visible in the left-hand window, while you scroll the right-handed window from side to side so that you can see all the figures.

To finish the job off, you need to complete the departmental totals and percentages for the two new departments. This time use the SmartIcons in the fourth line of the control panel.

- Make sure you are in the right hand window.

- Highlight cells B13 to B15. Now copy this by clicking on the Copy SmartIcon. Highlight cells C13 to E15, then click on the Paste SmartIcon.

Notice how not only the formulae have been copied, but also the formats (currency, decimals points, etc.) defined for the cells copied from.

At this stage you should have screen similar to that shown in **Screen dump 3.5**.

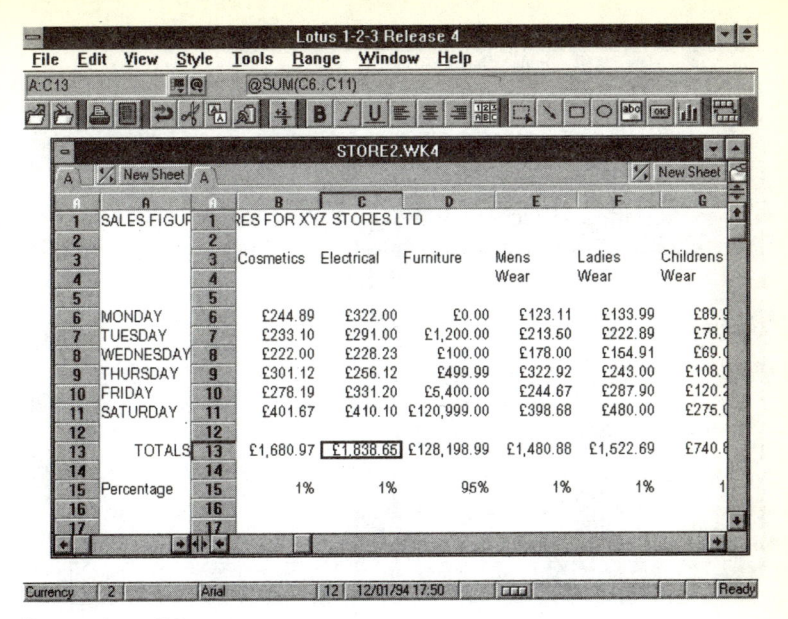

Screen dump 3.5

3.7 Using windows

Before proceeding any further, it is wise to save your latest efforts again so that nothing is lost.

- Click on the Save SmartIcon.

At this stage you will have saved the current version as STORE2 again. Remember that STORE, which was the earlier version, will also be on disk and is still open.

- Click on the Window option from the menu bar. Then select Tile.

The result should be similar to that shown in **Screen dump 3.6**.

You can hop freely between these two spreadsheets by clicking on them the same way as you hopped between the windows in the same spreadsheet.

LOTUS 1–2–3 WINDOWS

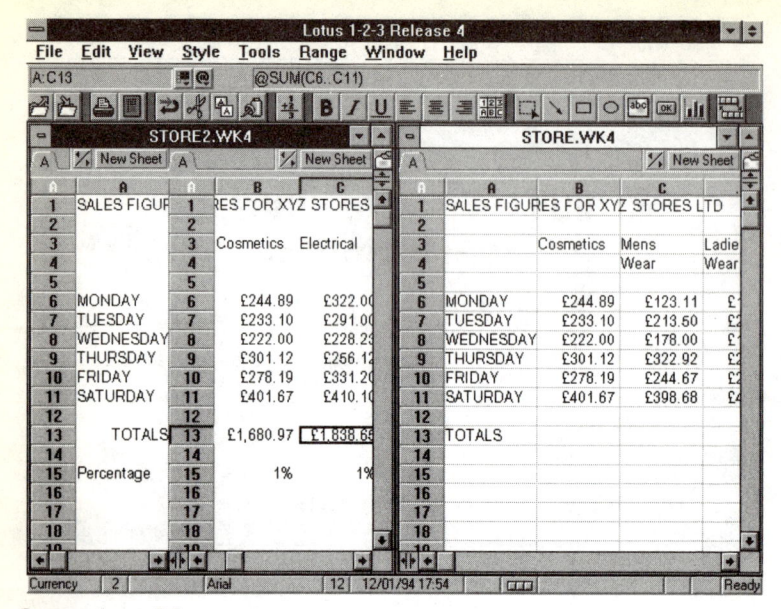

Screen dump 3.6

From the <u>W</u>indow option you can also select <u>C</u>ascade to see the spreadsheets one behind the other. In Chapter 9 you will see how Lotus 1-2-3 allows you to set up something similar to this by giving a spreadsheet a three-dimensional effect of multiple sheets within a single spreadsheet.

- Return to tiled Windows. Ensure that you are in the old spreadsheet – STORE.WK4.

- Close the file. The quickest way to do is to double click (i.e. press the left mouse button twice) on the minus sign in the left-hand button in the line containing the file title, in this case STORE.WK4.

This will leave your screen half empty. To fill the screen with your spreadsheet:

Either

Move the mouse pointer gently to the right-hand edge of the spreadsheet until you see it turn into a double-headed arrow. Then holding the mouse button down, drag the mouse to the right to fill your screen with the spreadsheet, rather like pulling a curtain across a rail.

— 52 —

Or
- Click on the maximise button in the right-hand corner of the line containing the file title.

3.8 Fonts, presentation and printing

The final section of this chapter will investigate the way you can alter the complete look of your spreadsheet. What you are able to achieve here may be a little restricted depending on the capabilities of your computer and printer.

To see more clearly what is going on, close the vertical window to have the whole spreadsheet showing on the screen.

- Click on View. Then select Clear Split.

If you are a Release 1 user then: click on Window. Then select Split. Then click on Clear, then on OK.

In order to see the whole spreadsheet on your screen you will need to alter the width of some of your columns.

Lotus 1-2-3 allows you to alter the column widths with your mouse in a similar way to the method of opening your spreadsheet across to fill the screen.

- Click on column letter A. The entire column is now highlighted. Move the mouse pointer carefully to the right edge of the box showing column letter A. The pointer turns into a black pointer.

- Holding the left mouse button down, drag the column heading to the right to widen the cell. When you let go of the mouse button, the new width will set accordingly.

Next you will have the opportunity to play around with the visual impact of what you have on the screen. This will vary in accordance with your system, so you will be left to experiment for yourself after a few preliminary instructions.

Look at **Screen dump 3.7** to get the idea of what can be achieved. Do not concern yourself if you are unable to achieve this; your system may be different from the one that was used for the purpose of writing this book.

LOTUS 1–2–3 WINDOWS

	A	B	C	D	E	F	G	H
1	**SALE$ FIGURES FOR XYZ STORES LTD**							
2								
3		Cosmetics	Electrical	Furniture	Mens	Ladies	Childrens	
4					Wear	Wear	Wear	TOTALS
5								
6	MONDAY	£244.89	£322.00	£0.00	£123.11	£133.99	£89.99	£913.98
7	TUESDAY	£233.10	£291.00	£1,200.00	£213.50	£222.89	£78.67	£2,239.16
8	WEDNESDAY	£222.00	£228.23	£100.00	£178.00	£164.91	£69.00	£952.14
9	THURSDAY	£301.12	£256.12	£499.99	£322.92	£243.00	£108.00	£1,731.15
10	FRIDAY	£278.19	£331.20	£5,400.00	£244.67	£287.90	£120.20	£6,662.16
11	SATURDAY	£401.67	£410.10	£120,999.00	£398.68	£480.00	£275.00	£122,964.45
12								
13	TOTALS	£1,680.97	£1,838.66	£128,198.99	£1,480.88	£1,622.69	£740.86	£135,463.04
14								
15	Percentage	1%	1%	95%	1%	1%	1%	

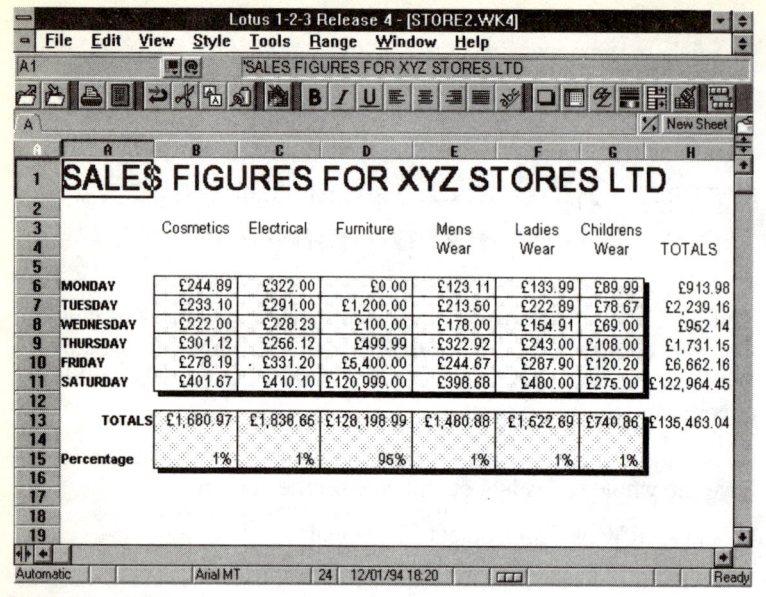

Screen dump 3.7

Most of the actions taken to achieve the above have been done with the options in the Style option from the menu bar. These are:

Fonts & Attributes
Lines & Color
Alignment
Gallery

[Release 1 is only slightly different, but all of the presentation aspects in **Screen dump 3.7** can be achieved. The options here are again available in the Style menu as:

Font: Changes font sizes and styles
Alignment: Positions text in cells
Border: Draws lines around cells and ranges
Color: Colours ranges
Shading: Shades ranges

First, you should discover the available fonts. This determines the style and size of letters and numbers. There are scores of fonts.

To change the font:

● Highlight the range of cells where you want the text to have a different font. For example, click on the row number 1. The entire row is now highlighted, including Sales Figures for XYZ Stores Ltd.

- Click on Style. Then select Font & Attributes.

The selection of fonts will be listed on your screen. The default face is Arial. Click on other Faces. The Sample box will show you how the font looks. The default size is 12 point, so the 24-point font will be twice the size, while the 10 point size is proportionately smaller.

- Click on a larger Size. (24 point, for example).
- Click on Arial Rounded MT Bold.
- Make any other alteration you wish and click on the OK button.

The effect should be instant.

To change alignment to centre the text where the columns headings are, for example:

- Highlight cells B3 to H4.
- Click on Style. Then select Alignment.
- Select Center in the Horizontal box in the Alignment dialogue box, and click on the OK button.

For boxed and shaded figures:

- Highlight cells B6 to G11.
- Click on Style. Then Lines & Color. [If you are a Release 1 user, Border.]
- You can select a different style for any of the lines by clicking on the appropriate boxes in the dialogue box. Pick a thin, thick or double line. Change the colour. Add shading.

The Gallery option in the Style menu contains pre-formatted styles that you can apply to any spreadsheet. These are well worth experimenting with.

Finally, print your spreadsheet.

- Highlight the range of cells that contains the whole spreadsheet.
- Click on the Print SmartIcon.

- Check the dialogue box has the range set to print the whole spreadsheet and, if any settings are wrong, alter them by entering the range to print to include the whole spreadsheet.
- Click on the OK button to start printing.

As an alternative to printing, you can always preview the spreadsheet on your screen.

- Click on the Print Preview SmartIcon. Then click on the OK button.

This will show you what the printed output should look like. Such a facility saves a lot of time as you do not have to wait for the printer to see if the effect is what you want. It also saves wasting paper.

Screen dump 3.8 shows the printed output produced landscape rather than portrait. In other words, the printed output would appear sideways down the paper. This is useful when the output is too wide for portrait mode.

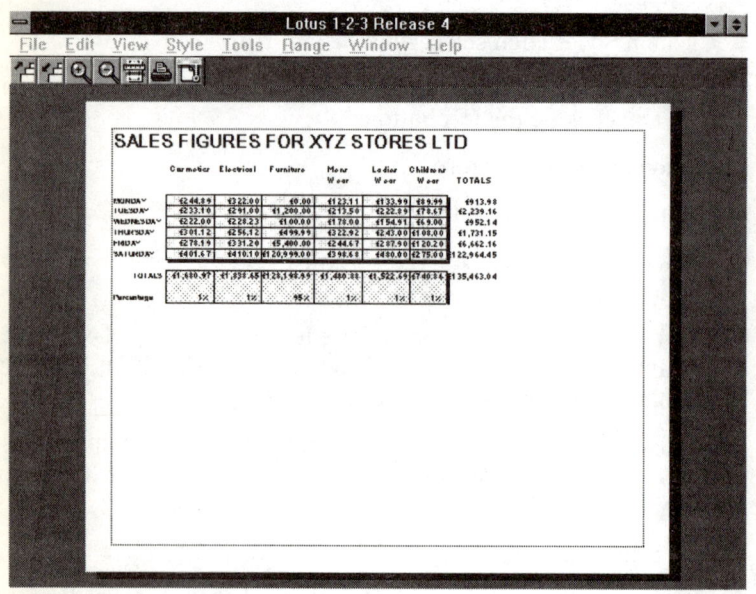

Screen dump 3.8

At the top of the preview screen are a number of new SmartIcons. The two left ones allow you to move from page to page. As you only have a single page, this is of no apparent use here. The two magnifying glasses allow you to zoom in and out on the sheet. The next one is the Page Setup icon; the printer icon prints the page; while the rightmost icon returns you to your spreadsheet.

- Click on the Page Setup icon.
- Click on Lan̲dscape in the Orientation box. Then click on the OK button.
- Inspect the new print preview and click on the Print icon to start printing.

Lotus 1-2-3's ability to give such a good visual presentation will be further developed in the next chapter when you go on to explore graphics. For now, spend some more time experimenting with what you have before you.

3.9 Chapter summary

This chapter has concentrated on how Lotus 1-2-3 commands are organised in a hierarchical menu structure with dialogue boxes for you to alter at will. Finding your way around menus will become easier though practice and experience.

In both file handling and printing, you will have examined only a part of what can be achieved. However, in both cases you have seen the important principles involved.

In this chapter you have:

- understood the menu bar, pull-down menus, and dialogue boxes;
- widened columns;
- used Save and Retrieve files in different ways;
- used Copy and Paste to copy both relative and absolute formulae;
- used Format ranges for currency and changed the currency symbol;
- used commands to insert columns;
- split screens to help you with extra large spreadsheets;

- used windows to inspect more than one spreadsheet at a time in Tile and Cascade;
- altered the physical appearance of a spreadsheet with different fonts, lines, colours and shading;
- previewed and printed a spreadsheet in landscape and portrait.

4
STATISTICS AND GRAPHS

4.1 Aims of this chapter

Lotus 1-2-3 has an extremely useful graphing facility for putting fine touches to your data. The purpose of this chapter is to familiarise you with these facilities and to develop your spreadsheet skills further.

Apart from being able to draw graphs, you will see that once the graph has been set up, it is instantly redrawn as the data changes. Later in the book, in Chapter 8, you will return to graphs and take the whole process a stage further.

A good deal of this chapter will require you to highlight ranges of cells with your mouse in order to make efficient use of the facilities contained in the pull-down menus or with the SmartIcons.

4.2 Reading the indicator

In the bottom line of the screen – the status bar – in the far right-hand corner appears the word 'Ready'. [In Release 1 it is on the third row from the top of the screen to the right.] This mode indicator changes as you perform different functions. Here are the most common indications:

Indicator	Mode
Edit	You pressed **F2 (EDIT)** to edit an entry; you are entering or editing text in a *text box*; or you made an incorrect entry.
Error	Lotus 1-2-3 is displaying a message. Choose Help or press **F1 (HELP)** to get Help; select OK to clear the message.
Label	You are entering a **label**.
Menu	You clicked the menu bar, or pressed **Alt** or **F10 (MENU)**; or in a dialog box, the the dotted box is in a list box or on a check box, option button, or command button.
Point	You are specifying a range before choosing a command, while working in a dialog box, or while entering a formula.
Ready	Lotus 1-2-3 is ready for you to enter data or choose a command.
Value	You are entering a value.
Wait	Lotus 1-2-3 is completing a command or process, such as saving a file.

Refer to the mode indicator if you get stuck.

4.3 Entering statistics

- Open a new spreadsheet by clicking on File, then selecting New. Look at **Screen dump 4.1** to see what you will be aiming at in terms of the data for the first exercise.

The spreadsheet shows the sales figures for a business selling five ranges of motor vehicles. The data on the spreadsheet will be used to give a graphical presentation of the Sales Income this business has secured over the January period.

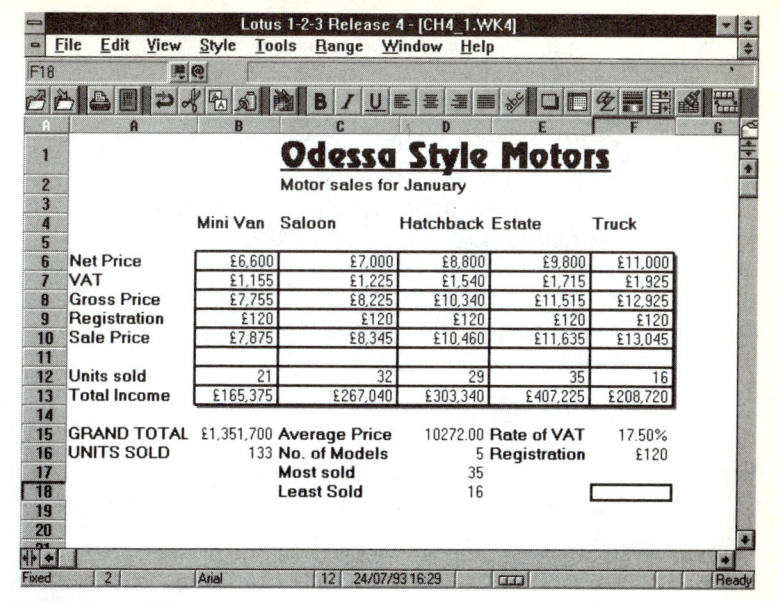

STATISTICS AND GRAPHS

![Screen dump showing Lotus 1-2-3 Release 4 spreadsheet]

	Mini Van	Saloon	Hatchback	Estate	Truck
Net Price	£6,600	£7,000	£8,800	£9,800	£11,000
VAT	£1,155	£1,225	£1,540	£1,715	£1,925
Gross Price	£7,755	£8,225	£10,340	£11,515	£12,925
Registration	£120	£120	£120	£120	£120
Sale Price	£7,875	£8,345	£10,460	£11,635	£13,045
Units sold	21	32	29	35	16
Total Income	£165,375	£267,040	£303,340	£407,225	£208,720

GRAND TOTAL £1,351,700 Average Price 10272.00 Rate of VAT 17.50%
UNITS SOLD   133   No. of Models 5   Registration £120
                         Most sold 35
                         Least Sold 16

Screen dump 4.1

Before moving on, think about how the data is to be set out and, in particular, which data areas are to be calculated by Lotus and which are to be typed in by you.

- Click on the maximise button for the spreadsheet area to give you more area to work with.

- Click on cell C1, type Odessa Style Motors, and press the **Enter** key.

- Click on Style, then select Font & Attributes.

- From the Font & Attributes dialogue box, select the following (use **Screen dump 4.2** as a guide):

- Click on Face Renfrew; Size 24; Attributes Underline.

- Click on the OK button.

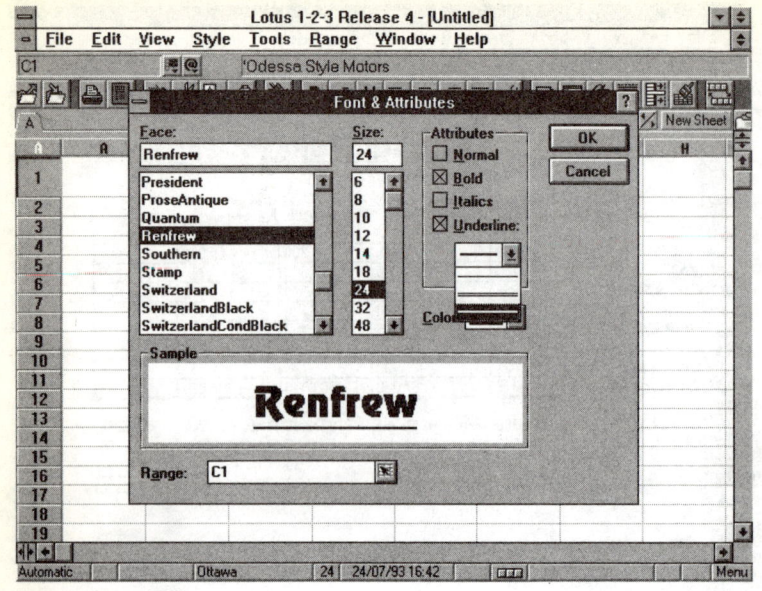

Screen dump 4.2

- Click on cell C2 and type Motor sales for January.

When entering the text into cells, the use of the backspace key allows you to delete characters while entering the text. Also, if the text is already on the spreadsheet and you want it altered, you can use the editing facilities of function key **F2** or your mouse to put it right. Altering text in cells will not alter the font settings you made earlier.

- Click on the SmartIcons to change the label in cell C2 to bold or in italic.

- Commence with the following entries:

In cell	Type	Press
B4	Mini Van	**Right Arrow**
C4	Saloon	**Right Arrow**
D4	Hatchback	**Right Arrow**
E4	Estate	**Right Arrow**
F4	Truck	**ENTER**

- Highlight cells B4 to F4.
- Click on the Bold SmartIcon to change them to bold.

STATISTICS AND GRAPHS

- Click on cell A6 and proceed with the following entries:

In cell	Type	Press
A6	Net Price	**Down Arrow**
A7	VAT	**Down Arrow**
A8	Gross Price	**Down Arrow**
A9	Registration Cost	**Down Arrow**
A10	Sale Price	**Down Arrow twice**
A12	Units sold	**Down Arrow**
A13	Total Income	**Down Arrow twice**
A15	GRAND TOTAL	**Down Arrow**
A16	UNITS SOLD	**Right Arrow twice, Up Arrow**
C15	Average Price	**Down Arrow**
C16	No. of Models	**Down Arrow**
C17	Most sold	**Down Arrow**
C18	Least sold	

Click on E15 Rate of VAT   **Down Arrow**

VAT is the acronym for Value Added Tax and is a percentage sales tax. A VAT rate of 10% will mean 10% is to be added to the price. Such rates alter from time to time, so it will be important to allow for these changes in spreadsheets that use them.

Having typed all this in, it should be apparent that Column A is too tight and needs widening.

- Highlight columns A to F.
- Click on Style, then Column Width. Click on Fit Widest entry, then the OK button.

Next you must type in numbers and formulae.

4.4 Good spreadsheet practice

Cell F15 will be used to store the current rate of VAT.

- Click on cell F15 and type in the current rate of 17.5%. Include the percentage sign.

Lotus 1-2-3 will convert this percentage to a fraction but you may need to format the cell so that it is read as a percentage.

- Make sure that only cell F15 is highlighted.

- Click on Style, then Number Format. Select Percent in the Format box, 0 in the Decimal places box, then click on the OK button. [If you are a Release 1 user click on the % SmartIcon.]

You will use this cell later to calculate the VAT to be charged on each car. This is good practice when designing a spreadsheet and it will be discussed further shortly.

- Type in the basic prices of the vehicles as whole numbers in cells B6 to F6.

The figures you are about to type in are currency, so you must change the Number Format to currency to 2 decimal places.

- Highlight cells B6 to F10.

- Click on Style, then Number Format, then Currency in the Format box, then click on the OK button.

- If the columns are too narrow, a row of ******* will warn you. The best way to make the columns fit is to highlight the whole spreadsheet – cells A4 to F18, then click on Style, then Column Width, then Fit widest entry, then click on the OK button.

Now it is time to calculate the amount of VAT payable on the Net Price of each vehicle. Cell F15 is an absolute cell for all vehicles. The VAT payable will be the price in the appropriate relative cell multiplied by the figure in absolute cell F15. If the rate of VAT were to alter, you can simply type the new rate in cell F15 (not forgetting to include the % symbol) and the VAT amounts will automatically be recalculated in row 7. This is what was meant by adapting good spreadsheet practice.

- Click on cell B7, type in the formula +B6*$F$15, and click on the tick icon.

Because the VAT cell is absolute, you can copy the formula to the rest of the vehicles and the VAT element will remain constant.

- With cell B7 highlighted, click on the Copy SmartIcon.

- Highlight cells C7 to F7, then click on the Paste SmartIcon.

Examine each of the formulae in the range of cells B7 to F7 to appreciate how the concept of relative and absolute cell locations works. Also, try changing the rate of VAT, to appreciate what is happening.

- Click on cell B8 and type in the formula +B6+B7. This will add VAT to the basic price.

- Now copy the formula in cell B8 to the range C8 to F8.

Row 9 will contain a registration cost, which will be the same for all vehicles. It would again be good practice to use a single cell to reference this cost.

- Click on cell E16, type in Registration and click on the tick icon.

- Change this text to bold to match the rest of the labels.

- Click on cell F16, type in the number 120.

- Make this cell a currency format.

- Click on cell B9 and type in the formula +$F$16.

- Now copy the formula in cell B9 to the range C9 to F9.

The formulae in the range of cells B9 to F9 contain only one single cell reference which has been fixed as absolute. You could just as easily have placed the number 120 into each cell. However, if the registration cost were to change, you would have six values to alter. Using this technique, you have only one cell value to alter.

You can now arrive at the sale price.

- Click on cell B10 and enter the formula +B8+B9 to add the Registration cost to the Gross Price.

- Copy the formula in cell B10 to the range C10 to F10.

- Now type in the units sold in row 12 for each of the six vehicles.

- Click on cell B13 and type in the formula +B10*B12, then click on the tick icon. This multiples the Sale Price with Units Sold to give Total Income.

- Now copy the formula in cell B13 to the range C13 to F13.

- Finally, format cells B13 to F13 as currency to zero places of decimals.

In **Screen Dump 4.1** the range of cells B6 to F13 has been boxed with a drop shadow and the grid lines have been removed. To do this

- Highlight cells B6 to F13.
- Click on Style, then Lines & Color.
- In the Border box in the Lines & Color dialogue box, click on Outline.
- Click on Designer frame, then click on the OK button.
- Click on View, then Set View Preferences. To remove the grid lines, click on Grid lines in the Show in Current file of the Set View Preferences dialogue box. Then click on the OK button.

The top part of your spreadsheet should now be complete. Save it. The next stages, before producing your first graph, will introduce you to a few new functions that you may well find useful in future.

4.5 Some new functions

Cells B15 and B16 will contain the total income and total units sold, respectively. These will be calculated using the function SUM, which you have used before.

- Click on cell B15.
- Click on the @ SmartIcon, then SUM.
- Highlight cells B13 to F13, then click on the tick icon.
- Click on Style, then Number Format, then Currency, then 0 Decimal places, then click on the OK button. If the column is not wide enough, click on column letter B to highlight the whole column and widen the column.

In cell D15 a function can be typed in that will calculate the average selling price based on the figures in cells B10 to F10. Lotus 1-2-3 will add up the five prices and divide by five. The function that will do this automatically is AVG.

- Click on cell D15.
- Click on the @ SmartIcon, then AVG.

STATISTICS AND GRAPHS

- Highlight cells B10 to F10, then click on the tick icon.
- Format this cell as currency, as before, this time to 2 decimal places.

Check with a calculator that this is correct.

Lotus 1-2-3 can also add up the number of cell entries in a range using the COUNT function. In cell D16 you want to total the number of models in the range B4 to F4. Although obvious at this stage, there may be an instance when you want to count entries in a much bigger range where some of the cells have no entries.

- Click on cell D16.
- Click on the @ SmartIcon, then on List All.
- Highlight cells B4 to F4, then click on the tick icon.
- In the @ Functions box, scroll until you see COUNT. Click on COUNT and then click on the OK button.

Finally, in cells D17 to D18 you want the maximum and minimum numbers, respectively, in the range B12 to F12.

- Click on cell D17.
- Click on the @ SmartIcon, then on List All.
- In the @ Functions box, scroll until you see MAX. Click on MAX and then click on the OK button.
- Highlight cells B12 to F12, then click on the tick icon.
- Do the same with cell D18, this time choosing MIN in the @ Functions dialogue box.
- Finally, check that you are satisfied with the formats of all numbers, column widths, display style and accuracy before going any further.

4.6 Creating a bar chart

This section shows how to produce from the spreadsheet a chart that shows the proportions of each vehicle type sold. All of the work in this section of the chapter will be carried out using the Tools option from the menu bar.

The basic order of activities that you will need to go through to produce a graph is as follows:

1 Highlight the area of the spreadsheet to be graphed.
2 Create the graph.
3 Define the ranges that are to make up the graph.
4 Select a graph type.

In this first example, you will generate a Bar graph that will show units sold for each vehicle type.

[If you are a Release 1 user then skip a few paragraphs, as graphs are created in a different way.]

- Click on Tools, then select Chart.
- The mouse pointer will change to a small graphics icon. Point this near the top corner of your spreadsheet and click the left mouse button.

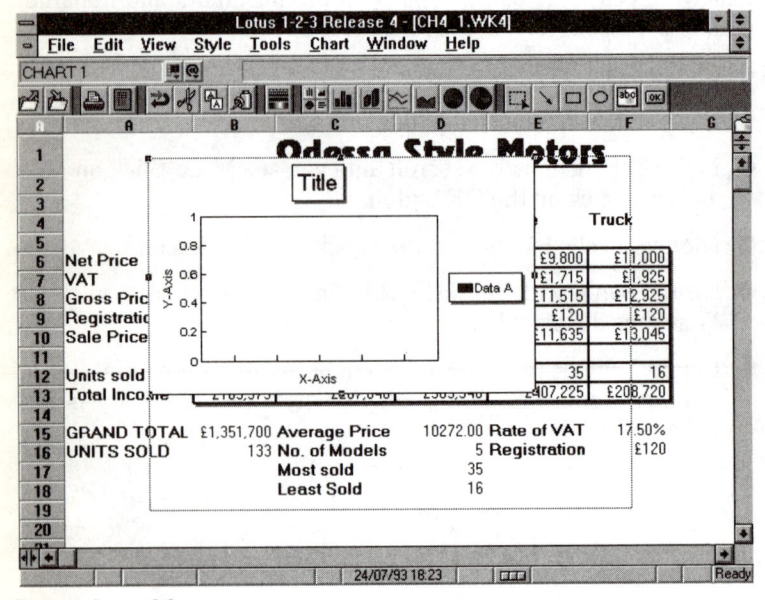

Screen dump 4.3

- Now position the mouse pointer on the bottom right corner of the graph area you created. The pointer will turn into a white cross. Holding down the left mouse button, drag the chart area downwards and to the right to create a larger graph.

Screen dump 4.3 illustrates the graph created and how it is being 'stretched' so that it appears bigger on the screen. Although the graph is covering the spreadsheet table, it will not cause any loss of data.

If you are a Release 1 user then:

- Click on Graph, then New.

- Enter the name ODESSA as your graph name. If you do not enter a name, then Lotus 1-2-3 will give the graph a default name of GRAPH1 if this is the first graph.

Your next goal will be to define the precise ranges that make up the graph. Look at the top of the screen and you will see that you now have a different menu bar. You also have a new set of SmartIcons.

- Familiarise yourself with the new screen.

- Click on Chart, then select Ranges.

This now leaves you with a dialogue box to complete in order to define the ranges. **Screen dump 4.4** shows the screen you will be given.

- Click on X-Axis labels in the Series box.

- Click on the Range box and type in B4..F4, then click on the OK button.

The X-Axis will always appear along the bottom of the pie chart on the horizontal axis unless you specify otherwise. The data ranges will appear on the left of the chart as a vertical axis. Hence, what you are plotting, in the form of a bar chart, is the Type of Motor vehicle along the X-Axis against Total Income along the vertical axis, sometimes referred to as the Y-Axis.

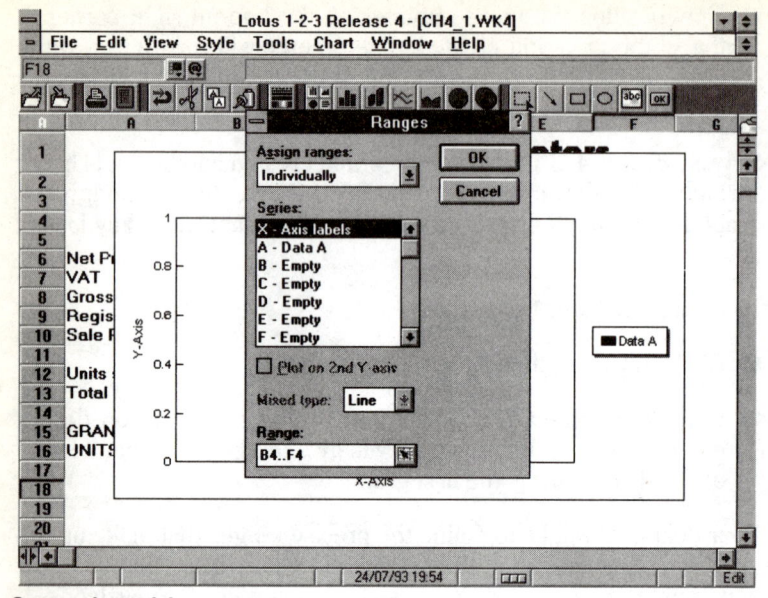

Screen dump 4.4

The X-Axis now shows the five different kinds of motor vehicles.

We want to plot the numbers of units sold (A Data range) against each vehicle type (the X data range). In your spreadsheet the cell range giving the number sold for each vehicle is B12 to F12.

(For this chapter, this will be the only data plotted and so will be the only series.)

- Click on Chart, then select Ranges.

- Click on A-Data A in the Series box, type in B12..F12 in the Range box, and click on the OK button.

You have asked Lotus 1-2-3 to plot the number of units sold against vehicle type. The X Axis represents the types of vehicles in the range of cells from B4..F4 and the Y axis represents the numbers sold in the range B12..F12.

Depending on the version of Lotus 1-2-3 you are using, you will have either a line chart or a 2-D bar chart. The next stage will be to alter this chart to a 3-D bar chart.

- Click on Chart, then Type.

Screen dump 4.5 shows that you have a selection of graph types to choose from in the Types box. Each type activates a new collection of icons. For the purpose of this section of the chapter you should start with the 3-D bar chart because this is the simplest.

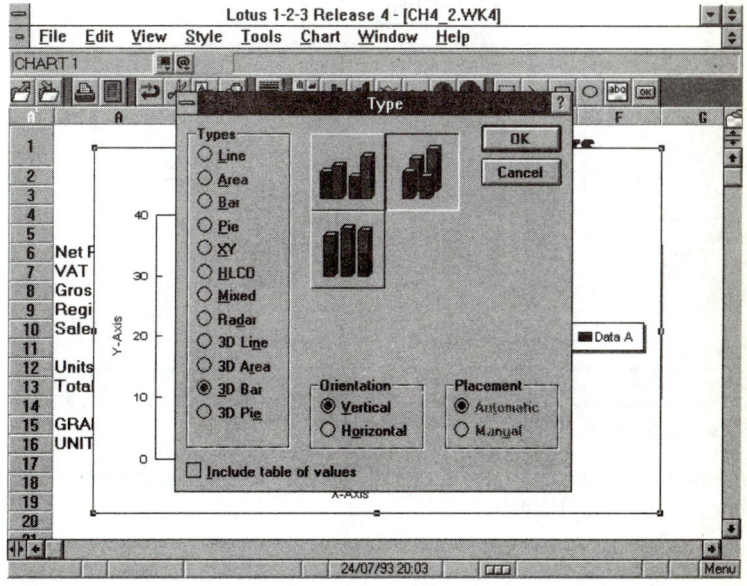

Screen dump 4.5

- Click on 3D Bar in the Types box of the Type dialogue box, then click on the OK button.

Many other graph types will not be appropriate for this kind of spreadsheet example. Chapter 8 will give you the chance to work with many of the other graph types and with different kinds of data that are more appropriate.

Release 1 users will find that many of the types listed above are not available. This will prevent you from being able to work through the rest of this chapter.

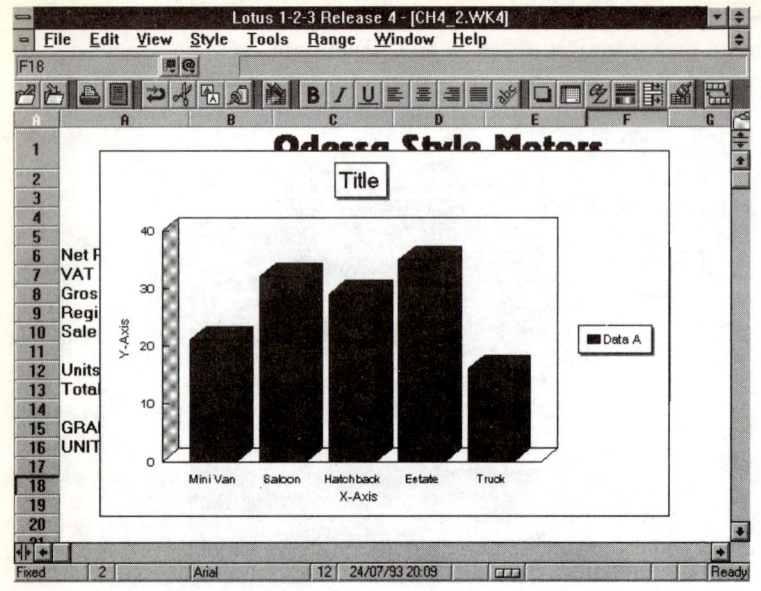

Screen dump 4.6

As an alternative to this you can click your mouse button on the 3D bar graph SmartIcon.

Screen dump 4.6 shows result you should get.

It was suggested earlier that if you change your data, in this case the number of units sold, then the graph would change to match the new data. It is now worth doing this to see the effect.

Release 4 users should click on the graph and move it down the screen by holding down the left-hand mouse button until both bar chart and the Units Sold line of the spreadsheet are in view.

[Release 1 users should hold down the **Ctrl** key and press function key **F6**.]

● Now change the number of units sold in row 12:

Cell	Units sold
B12	51
C12	101
D12	14
E12	31
F12	62

STATISTICS AND GRAPHS

You will see the bar chart change as soon as you type in the new values and press the **Enter** key.

[For release 1, click on Graph, then View. You have to choose which graph you wish to view from the dialogue box. As you probably have just the one graph (ODESSA), this will appear as the default. Click on ODESSA and then click on the OK button. At this stage, experiment a little with the numbers and moving between the graph and spreadsheet to see the effect.]

The graph is technically sound, but to make it look more professional, you can add labels and a title.

- Click on the graph area. Then double click on the Title box in the graph. You will see the Headings dialogue box.

- Type into the top two boxes:

    Line 1 (the title) :   ODESSA STYLE MOTORS
    Line 2 (the subtitle) :   Sales for January

    then click on the OK button.

Next you should label the axes appropriately, noting that the horizontal axis is the X Axis and the vertical axis the Y axis.

- Click on the words X-Axis in the graph. Square boxes will appear in the four corners. Double click the mouse and you will see the X-Axis dialogue box. The Axis title box will be highlighted, so double click on the box and type in the words: Vehicle type, then click the OK button.

- Click on the words Y-Axis in the graph, then double click. The Y-Axis dialogue box will appear. Double click on the Axis title box and type in: Number of Units Sold.

- Finally, double click on the Data A box. You want to delete this, so click on the Legend entry box and press **Delete** until the box is empty. Then click on the OK button.

Screen dump 4.7 shows the graph with the appropriate title and labels on the axes.

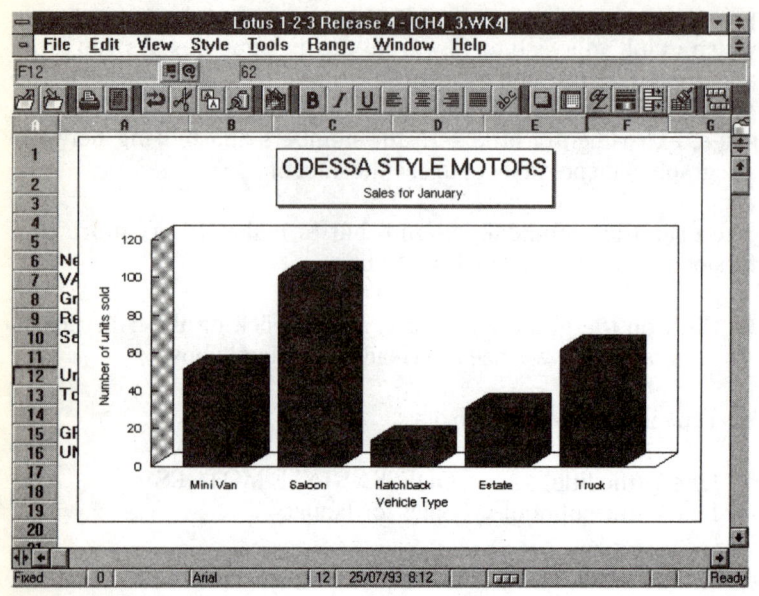

Screen dump 4.7

Finally, you will need to name your graph for later use. [Release 1 will already have done this in order to create the graph in the first place.] First click on the area of the screen showing the graph.

● Click on Chart, then Name. You will see that the Name dialogue box will have given your graph or bar chart the default name CHART 1. Click on the Chart name box and type in the name: ODESSA.

In chapter 8, you will create a collection of graphs, all in the same spreadsheet. Lotus 1-2-3 allows you to have many graphs defined in a spreadsheet. It distinguishes between the different graphs by giving each one a unique name. These 'named' graphs will, therefore, become part of the spreadsheet when it is saved or opened.

4.7 Changing the graph type

Changing the graph type is simple. Click on the Pie SmartIcon. **Screen dump 4.8** shows a resulting pie chart.

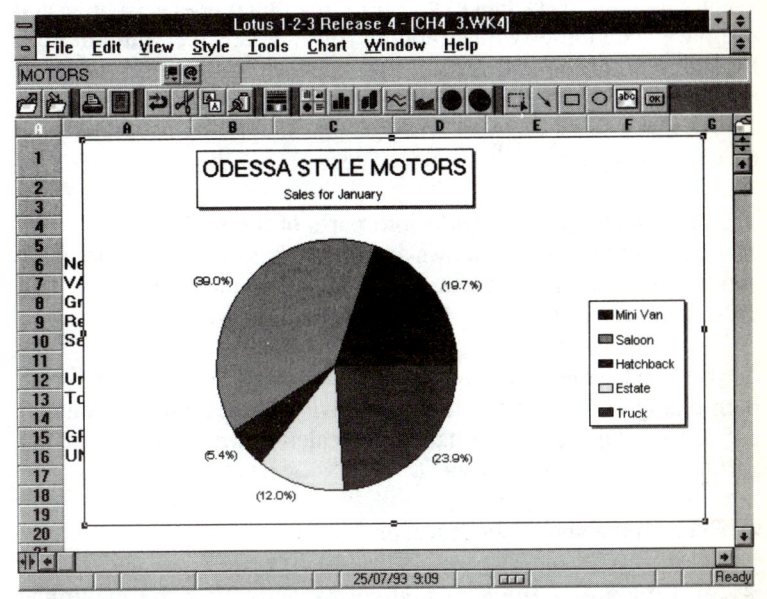

Screen dump 4.8

The pie chart shows the same data as the bar chart but this time the segments give the proportions of total sales. Observe that Lotus 1-2-3 shows against each segment the percentage each segment represents of the whole. Add these percentages together to get 100%.

In both graphs, Lotus 1-2-3 scales the elements to fill up a reasonable proportion of the screen. You can control this yourself, and this topic will be covered in Chapter 8.

Experiment with the other SmartIcons; many of them, however, will not be appropriate. Further graph types will be developed in Chapter 8 along with many other facilities that are available with Lotus 1-2-3 graphics.

4.8 Release 1: graph insertion

In this section of this chapter, you will learn how to place your graph into your spreadsheet and print the outcome. Up to now, you will have seen either your graph or your spreadsheet, but not both together. Before inserting your spreadsheet you can get a look at both graph and spreadsheet together.

- Click on Windows, then select Tile.

This allows you to work with both parts of the spreadsheet freely. You can hop between windows as you did before. On this occasion you are looking at two parts of the same spreadsheet rather than different ones.

As you hop between the two the menu bars and SmartIcon bars will both change to reflect the different environments. You will further notice that the graph size has been scaled down to fit the smaller part of screen available to see it.

- Click on the spreadsheet screen.

- First maximise the spreadsheet by activating the maximise button in the top right corner of the spreadsheet.

The graph will eventually be placed starting at cell C15, currently occupied by some statistical details. Your next task, therefore, is to move these to another position.

- Click on cell C15 and highlight the range C15..D18.

- Click on Edit, then select Cut. This will place the range into the clipboard and remove it from your spreadsheet.

- Now click on cell A17, click on Edit, then select Paste.

You will notice that not only have all the cell contents been preserved, but the formulae have been rewritten to compensate for the changes in cell locations.

STATISTICS AND GRAPHS

- Now move the range E15..F16 in the same way to start at cell A21.

Again, not only have the formulae in the cells you have moved been preserved, but the formula further up the spreadsheet has been altered to allow for the change in location of the VAT and Registration figures.

To insert the graph into the spreadsheet:

- Highlight the range of cells A19 to F36, which is where the graph is to go.

- Click on Graph, then select Add to Sheet.

This entire spreadsheet, with graph, can now be printed in exactly the same way as you printed the spreadsheet.

4.9 Customizing the spreadsheet

At this stage, it is worth looking at some of the options available for altering the appearance of your graph.

- Click on the chart area to make the chart area active.

- Now click the *right* mouse button to reveal a small menu.

- Click on Lines & Color from this menu.

If you look at **Screen dump 4.9** you will see that you now have the option of altering the interior of your graph, the edges and the frame.

- Click on the Designer frame box and select a frame and frame colour that appeal to you.

- Experiment with some of the other options.

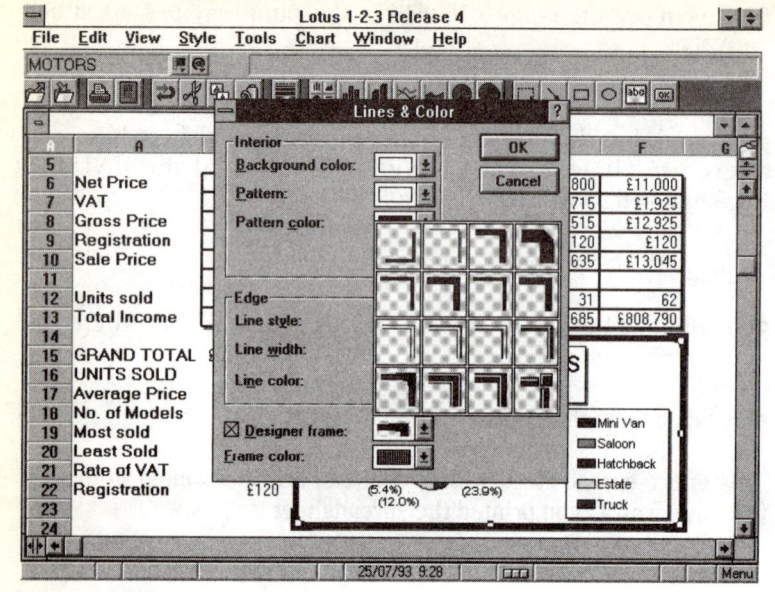

Screen dump 4.9

- Click on the OK button and inspect your work. If it is not suitable, then return to the Lines & Color box and make the necessary alterations. Do not concern yourself about getting an exact match to those in the screen dumps.

Your next task will be to position the graph in the spreadsheet so that it will print neatly. To do this you will move lines from the spreadsheet to make way for the graph.

- Highlight cells C15 to D18.

- Now position the mouse on the edge of the highlighted range so that a small hand appears.

- With the hand on the screen, hold down the left mouse button. The fist clenches to indicate you have grabbed the cell. Slowly drag the entire block to a position under "Units Sold" in cells A16 to B16, and let go of the mouse button.

Not only have all cell contents been preserved, but the formulae have been changed to compensate for the moved cell locations.

- Now move cells E15 to F16 in the same way, to fit under "Least Sold" in cells A20 to B20.

Not only have the formulae in the cells you have moved been preserved, but the formulae elsewhere in the spreadsheet have been altered to allow for the changes in location.

Now move the graph:

- Click on the graph, hold down the left mouse button, and drag the entire chart so that its top left corner is positioned at cell C15.
- Resize the chart to best fit the page.

The graph should now be below the table similar to that shown in **Screen dump 4.10**.

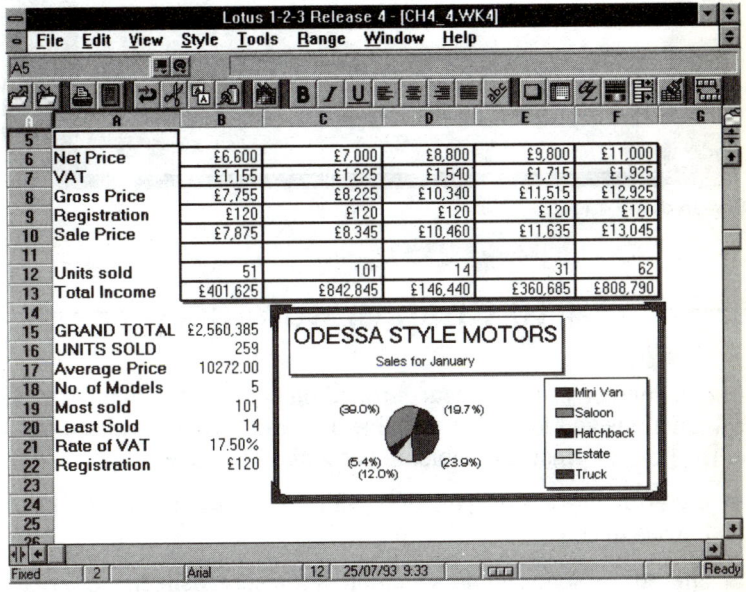

Screen dump 4.10

To finish this chapter, preview the page to be printed and then print it.

- Click on the Print Preview SmartIcon, then click on Current Worksheet in the Preview box, and click on the OK button.

Screen dump 4.11 illustrates what you should see as a preview and so what will appear on the printout. The Print Preview has been set up for landscape orientation using Page Setup.

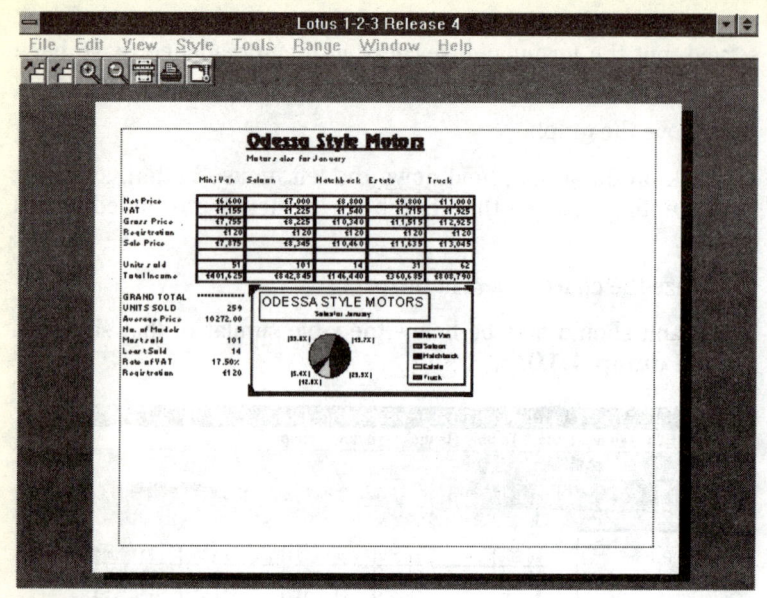

Screen dump 4.11

4.10 Chapter summary

In this chapter you have concentrated on some of the many statistical functions and formulae available in Lotus 1-2-3 and utilised a few of the graph formats available. In particular you have:

- covered more work on text, values, formulae and function entries to cells;
- altered the style and presentation of the spreadsheet;
- copied ranges of cells with absolute and relative formula contents;
- produced a graph;
- labelled the graph;
- generated different graphs;
- moved ranges of cells around the spreadsheet;
- positioned a graph in the spreadsheet.

5
STYLE AND PRESENTATION

5.1 Aims of this chapter

This chapter concentrates on a number of issues regarding the set up of your spreadsheet and how to present your data in a form that is appropriate to the problem in hand. It will also explain the good practice of naming areas of your spreadsheet.

The first part of the chapter is based on a stock system set out in tabular form showing data in a number of different formats.

The second part of the chapter is based on a sales report showing sales and profit figures in a simple table with a chart and a significant amount of text. The text will be manipulated in a way similar to a word processor and will show you how you can import text from a word processing package.

5.2 Styles for data

As a starting-point examine the spreadsheet in **Screen dump 5.1**, which lists items of stock showing Stock Code, Description, Number in stock, Cost Price and Selling Price.

LOTUS 1–2–3 WINDOWS

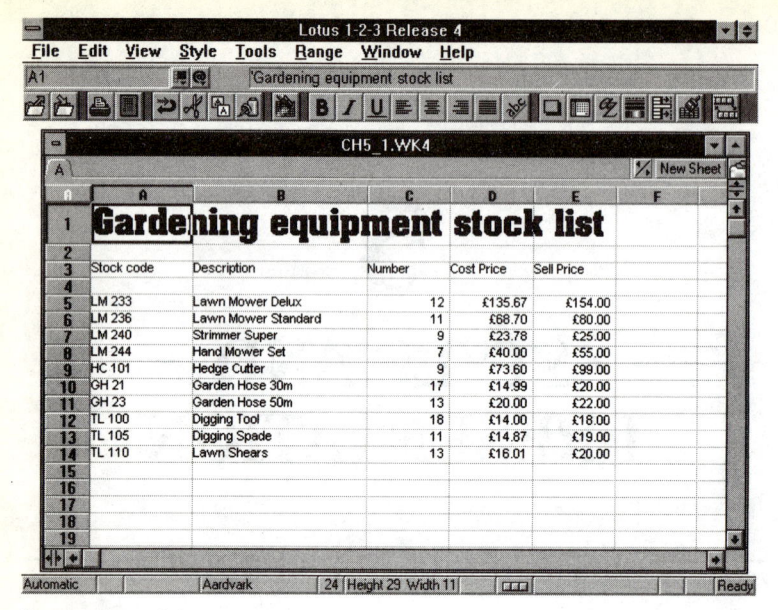

Screen dump 5.1

- In order to get started, type in the data in **Screen dump 5.1** in a new spreadsheet.

- Click on the white A in the left-hand file of the row headings at the top of the column numbers. This will highlight the entire spreadsheet. In the bottom status line, click on the 12, the default Font size, and then click on 10, to make all the characters in the spreadsheet smaller.

- If you have not already done so, widen column B by clicking on the dividing line between column headings B and C and pulling the columns apart.

- Give the title "Gardening equipment stock list" a more prominent size and face. Highlight the range that contains the heading, then click on Arial in the bottom status line and choose a different Face.

- The numbers in columns D and E are currency. Highlight cells D5 to E14, click on the right mouse button, then select Number Format.

- From the Number Format dialogue box select the Currency option and set the numbers to 2 decimal places.

5.3 Date formats

In this section and the next, you will examine in more detail some of the other formats available in Lotus 1-2-3. You now have enough information to type in to the spreadsheet stock details about value and possible profit.

- Click on cell F3 and type in the label Stock Value.
- Now click on cell F5 and type in the formula +C5*D5.

The formula in cell F5 multiplies Stock Quantity with Cost Price. Do not copy this formula yet, as you will do that later.

- Click on cell G3 and type in the label Unit Profit.
- Now click on cell G5 and enter the formula +E5−D5.

The formula in cell G5 subtracts Cost Price from Selling Price to give the unit profit. Again, do not copy this formula yet.

- Click on cell H3 and type in the label Gross and in cell H4 type in the label Profit.
- Now click on cell H5 and type in the formula +C5*G5.

The formula in cell H5 multiples Stock Quantity with Unit Profit to give the Gross Profit per line.

- Format the range F5 to H5 as currency, to 2 decimal places. [Release 1 users, highlight the range and select the % SmartIcon.]

At this stage, you now have three formulae that can be copied down the spreadsheet in one operation.

- Highlight cells F5 to H5.
- With the arrow on the highlighted cells, click on the right mouse button, select Copy, to copy the formulae to the clipboard (or click on Edit in the menu bar, then Copy).
- Highlight the destination range: cells F6 to H14.

- With the arrow on the highlighted cells, click on the right mouse button, select Paste (or click on Edit in the menu bar, then Paste).

Notice how the formats have also copied through.

- Click on cell E10, type in: 10, and press the **Enter** key. Observe how the Unit Profit appears in brackets to indicate a loss and how the formats have remained as currency.

At this stage your spreadsheet should be fairly full. The next stage is to type in a date when the stock was received. You will also create a column to store the number of days the stock has been held. In doing this, you will learn a little about the Lotus 1-2-3 date function and how it can be used.

The date in the date function appears in the format: @DATE (94, 6, 20) where:

94 is the year 1994;
6 is the 6th month : June;
20 is the day in the month.

You are able to enter a date into a cell but will not see it appear in an immediately recognisable format, as you will now find out.

- Click on cell I3 and type in the label Last and in cell I4 type in the label Delivery.

- Now click on cell I5 and enter the date function with a date as @DATE (94, 6, 19).

What will appear in the cell is the number 34505. This is the number of days between 1 January 1900 and the date that was entered (6 June 1994). This may seem odd at first, but it will allow you to perform some useful calculations. However, to make sense of it you will need to alter its format.

- Highlight the whole range where the dates are to appear, ie. cells I5 to I14.

- With the arrow on the highlighted cells, click on the right mouse button, select the Number Format option. [For Release 1 this will be Range and then Format.]

- Scroll through the formats in the Format box and click on the format 31-Dec-93, then click on the OK button.

The date format indicates how the date will now appear.

Although only the one cell has an actual date in it, Lotus 1-2-3 allows you to prepare in advance the cell format for future input.

- Type in the following dates in their respective cells:

Cell	Date
I6	@DATE (94, 6, 20)
I7	@DATE (94, 6, 10)
I8	@DATE (94, 6, 15)
I9	@DATE (94, 6, 20)
I10	@DATE (94, 6, 10)
I11	@DATE (94, 6, 15)
I12	@DATE (94, 6, 20)
I13	@DATE (94, 6, 10)
I14	@DATE (94, 6, 15)

As you enter these dates you should see the requested format appear.

Column J will hold the number of days between the date of the last delivery and the current date. What you need, therefore, is a facility whereby the computer can calculate this for you. The function that does this is @TODAY.

- Click on cell A16 and type in the label Date.
- Now click on cell B16 and type in @TODAY.
- Now format the cell with the date option, as before.

Providing your computer has the correct date and time set, you should see today's date. If the date is wrong, then enter today's date in the cell, using the date function. The benefit of the TODAY function over the DATE is that if you return to the spreadsheet on another day, the date is altered automatically.

You now have the facility to enter the days lapsed between a delivery and today for each item of stock.

- Click on cell J3 and type in the label Days and in cell J4 the label Lapsed.
- Click on cell J5 and type in the formula +$B$16−I5.

This calculates the number of days from today to the date of the last delivery. Notice also how the cell location B16 in the formula has been set as an absolute.

● Now copy the formula in cell J6 to the cells J6 to J14.

At this stage, you should have a spreadsheet similar to that of **Screen dump 5.2**.

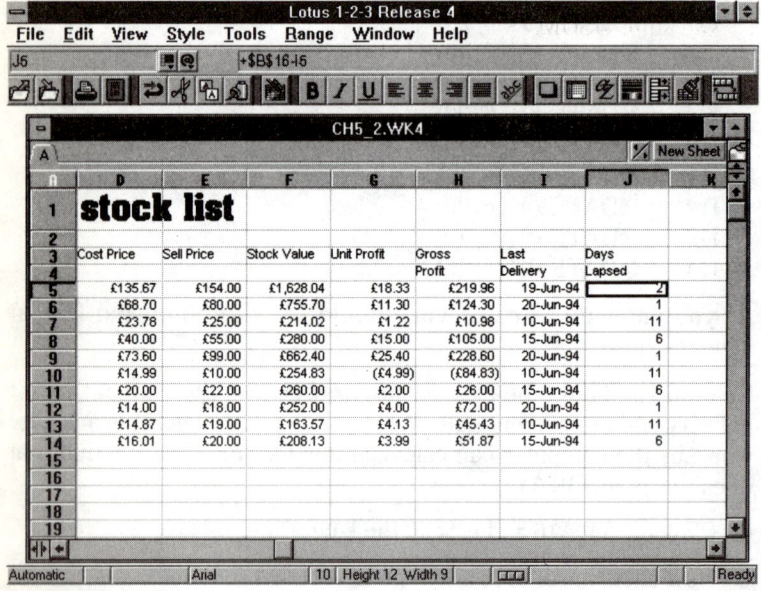

Screen dump 5.2

5.4 Naming ranges

This section will show you how you can give a range of cells a distinct name rather than identifying it by its cells. It is much easier to remember the name of a range rather than the co-ordinates of a range. It is also a useful way of documenting what is on your spreadsheet.

● Highlight cells F5 to F14.

● With the arrow on the highlighted cells, click on the right mouse button, and select Name.

- In the Name box in the Name dialogue box, type in Stock Value and click on the OK button. [If you are a Release 1 user you will need to select the Create option and give it the name 'Stock Value'.]
- Now click on cell F16 and type in the formula that will calculate the sum: @SUM (Stock Value).

Instead of using the range references in the formula, you were able to use the range name. This will make the spreadsheet much easier to follow if you return to it at a later stage and examine the formulae.

- Highlight cells G5 to G16.
- Give the range the title Unit Profit.

You will notice that the Existing named ranges panel contains a list of range names already in existence; these are automatically written upper case despite the fact that they may have been written in upper and lower case. You cannot have two ranges with the same name.

- Highlight cells H5 to H16.
- Give the range the title Gross Profit.
- Click on cell H16 and type in the formula to calculate the sum: @SUM (Gross Profit).
- Highlight cells J5 to J16.
- Give the range the title Days Lapsed.

You now have a collection of these range names and it is always a good idea to keep a list of them somewhere. Fortunately, Lotus 1-2-3 will do this for you.

- Click on Range, then Name. Highlight the range name DAYS LAPSED in the Existing named ranges box.
- Now click on the Use Labels button, then click on the OK button.

Screen dump 5.3 shows the screen you should have had when selecting a named range to use. When you return to the spreadsheet the selected range remains highlighted. This can be particularly useful when your spreadsheet becomes large.

LOTUS 1-2-3 WINDOWS

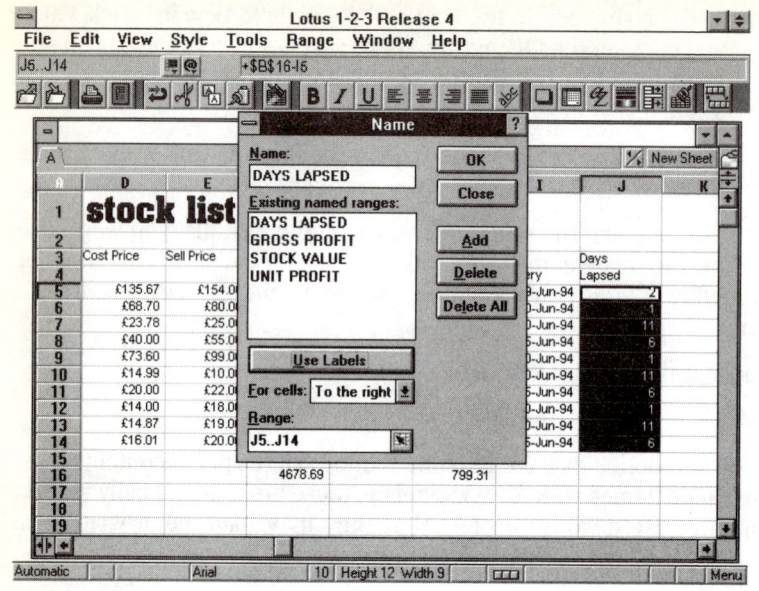

Screen dump 5.3

[If you are a Release 1 user then:

- Click on cell B18.
- Click on Range, then Name, then Paste Table.

This will create a table of ranges with names for you.]

As a final illustration of their use, do the following:

- Click on cell E17, type in the label Averages, and in cell G17 the function @AVG (Unit Profit).
- Click on cell J16 and type in the function @AVG (Day Lapsed).
- Format the range F16 to H17 to currency as before.
- Format cell J17 to Number Format Fixed, to 0 decimal places.

—— 5.5 Summarising the formats ——

- Highlight the cells A3 to J4. Click on Style, then Alignment.

— 88 —

- In the Horizontal box click on Center and then click on the OK button.

You can align data within a cell or across the columns of a range. Select the Range and then click on the appropriate box. Under Horizontal you have the following:

General   Aligns labels to the left and values to the right.

Left   Aligns data to the left.

Right   Aligns data to the right.

Center   Centres data.

Evenly spaced   Stretches data within the cell by expanding the spaces between letters and words.

Across columns   For ranges only: aligns data in the leftmost cell over the columns within the range, according to your selection under Horizontal.

There are also SmartIcons to centre, right align and left align data highlighted in cells or ranges.

You have now made use of most of the Number Format options from the Style pull-down menu. The following are available:

Fixed   Displays numbers to a specified number of decimal places, a minus sign for negatives, and a leading zero for decimal values.

Scientific   Numbers are displayed in the form of e.g. 4.733E−2. This scientific form is similar to that available on most calculators.

Currency   Currency symbols are used as prefix or suffix, depending how you have determined it. Thousands are separated with commas. Negative numbers are bracketed.

Comma   Commas are used to separate thousands. Negative numbers are bracketed.

General   The default format: numbers are displayed with a minus sign for negatives, no thousand separators and no trailing zeros to the right of the decimal point.

+/−	This converts numbers to rows of + (plus) or − (minus). The number 5 would be displayed as +++++ while −3 could appear as −−−.
Percent	This multiplies a stored number by 100, sets it to a specified number of decimal places and places a % sign after it.
Text	This displays the cell formulae rather than their computed values.
Hidden	This allows you to hide cell contents from display without actually removing them from the spreadsheet.
Automatic	If you type in, say $1000, Lotus 1-2-3 assigns the Currency format; if you type 8/25/93, it assigns a date format.
Label	Displays new entries as labels by automatically adding a label-prefix character that corresponds to the alignment set on Style Worksheet Defaults. Displays existing numbers in General format.

There then follows a set of date formats and then a set of time formats.

5.6 Protecting ranges of cells

This final section dealing with your current spreadsheet will show you how to protect ranges of cells from being written over. In this case, you will name the range of cells that can be altered by a user and then protect the rest of the spreadsheet from a user writing over them.

The different versions of Lotus 1-2-3 do have different ways of performing the protection. Release 1 users should skip the next few instructions to the heading "Protection with Release 1".

● Highlight cells C5 to H14.

- Click on Style, then Protection. Click on the keep data unprotected box.
- Click on the OK button.
- Click on File, then Protect.
- Click on Seal file, in the File protection box, then click on the OK button.

You will now be asked for a password. As you enter the password an asterisk will appear for each character, thereby concealing what you are entering. The purpose of this is to ensure someone cannot see your password being entered. In addition to the password, you have to put exactly the same text into the Verify box. If they differ in the slightest way, Lotus 1-2-3 will not seal the file.

- Type in ODESSA in the Password box. (All caps!)
- Type in ODESSA in the Verify box, then click on the OK button.
- Now try to change the Number Format or Font.

Lotus 1-2-3 will allow you to alter the data in the cells in this range. Styles, however, are protected.

The only real problem you could have here is forgetting your password.

To release the protection you would click on File, then Protect. However, Lotus 1-2-3 will ask for your password before it unseals the file for you.

[Protection with Release 1

- Highlight cells C5 to H14.
- Click on Range, then Name, and select the Create option.
- Type in the name Stock details.

If you want to update the table of named ranges, then you can always go back to cell B18, click on Range, then Name, and then select Paste Table.

- Click on Worksheet, then Global settings.
- Click on Protection, then click on the OK button.

This will set the whole spreadsheet into protect mode. You are now unable to alter anything on the spreadsheet. To alter details you need to Unprotect the cells:

- Click on Range, then Unprotect.
- Type in the range name Stock Details.

The part of the spreadsheet that is unprotected will be coloured in a lighter shade which indicates that you can now alter any data in this range of cells. This still protects many of the cells from being written over. Try to type in data in these protected cells.

You do not need to leave the formulae in columns F, G and H unprotected. In fact, the only part of the spreadsheet you really want left unprotected is that part where numbers are to be typed in.

- Highlight these cells and click a Range, then Protect to set these cells back as protected.

By protecting cells, you simply prevent alterations to the formulae in the cells, not their results.]

- Before the next sections, save your work giving the spreadsheet the name GARDEN.
- Now erase the spreadsheet. Click on File, then Close. A blank spreadsheet should appear.

5.7 Presenting text

This second part of the chapter looks at dealing with text in more detail and examines some of the presentation qualities available in the Lotus 1-2-3 package. The concentration is very much on visual appearance.

In a new spreadsheet you will type in details concerning an improvement in sales with the following sections:

   A heading
   A box of text
   A graph
   A table

First, the heading:

- In cell A1 type: Bumper Sales Year and Profits.
- Now use the font and size buttons to enhance the heading, and then underline it.

Typing in the text which follows will prove a little more interesting. You will type in just two cells to start with and then get Lotus 1-2-3 to rearrange it in a range of cells. Observe what appears in **Screen dump 5.4**.

The text typed into cell A3 is much longer than can appear on one line and appears to go off the screen. You can type up to 256 characters in a single line.

- Type the following text in cell A3 remembering not to press the Enter key:

    As shown in the graph, we are pleased to report a significant increase in our sales for the last year. As you can see from the graph, sales are up and, in addition to this, we are pleased to report that this has resulted in a corresponding rise in

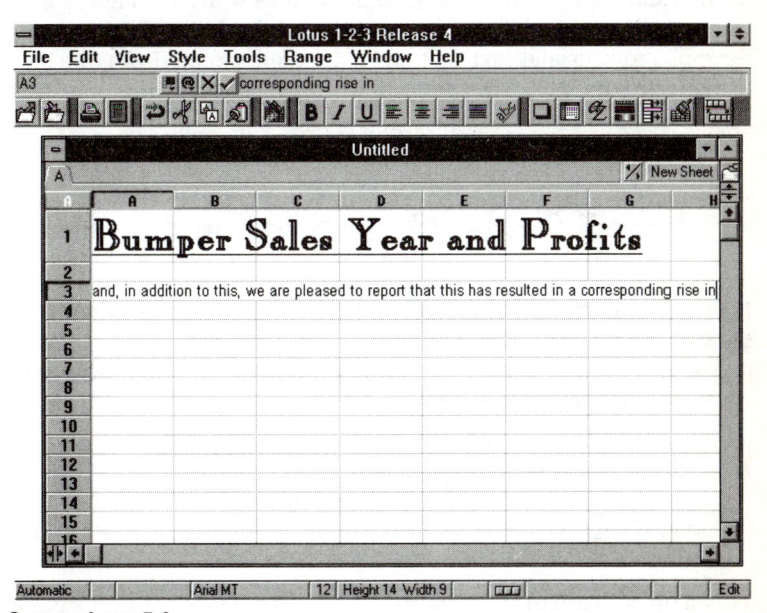

Screen dump 5.4

Note how the text is now off the screen. You can also see that the control panel grows as words fill the box.

- Type in the following text in cell A4 as you did in cell A3:

    profits. We are also pleased to report that this rise over the last year is expected to continue into next year and even into the foreseeable future.

You will now ask Lotus 1-2-3 to take this text and reformat it into a range of cells to make all the text visible.

- Highlight cells A3 to D13 and Enter.

[● If you are a Release 1 user then click on Range, then Justify.]

If you are a Release 4 user then you must activate a different menu known as the Classic menu. Follow the next three steps:

- Activate the classic menu with the / (forward slash) key.
- Select Range then Justify from the menu by pressing the J key.

The text will now have been reformatted into this range and no text should go over this specified range. You will also notice that the single range defined must contain the text as well as being the area wanted. This can be particularly helpful when you want, for example, to reformat text that takes up a full screen down one side of the spreadsheet. This will allow you to have columns of text similar to that of newspapers.

5.8 Search and replace

If you use a word processing package, then you will already be familiar with this facility. Lotus 1-2-3 can scan through a range of text searching for a word (or string of characters), and replace it. As an example you can get Lotus 1-2-3 to replace the word "report" with "announce":

- Highlight cells A3 to D11.
- Click on Range, then Name, type in article in the Name box, then click on the OK button.

This names that part of the spreadsheet where the text is stored. It can be referenced later.

STYLE AND PRESENTATION

- Click on Edit, then Find & Replace.

You will see a series of boxes in the Find & Replace dialogue box.

- Type in ARTICLE in the Search through: Selected range box to indicate where the text is on the spreadsheet.
- In the Search for box type: report
- Click the Replace with box and type: announce
- The Include box [Search Through in Release 1] should have Both activated.

At this point you will see **Screen dump 5.5**.

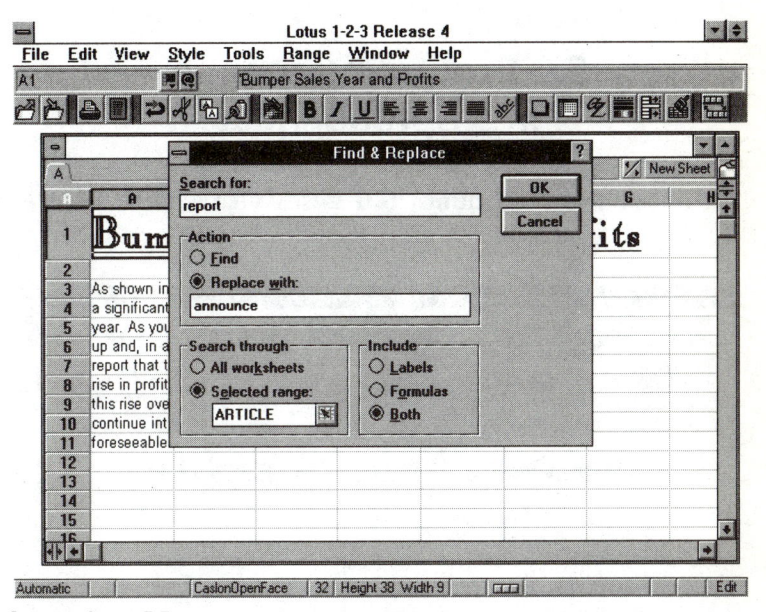

Screen dump 5.5

- Click on the OK button.

A set of buttons indicates one of three actions that can now be taken:

Find Next: Highlights the first occurrence of "report" without replacing the current occurrence.

Replace: Locates the first occurrence of the string "report" and replaces it with "announce".

Replace All: Replaces all occurrences of "report" with "announce" in the specified range, then returns to Ready mode.

- Click on Replace All.

You will now observe that all occurrences of "report" have been replaced with "announce".

You can use this facility simply to locate words in a long piece of text without replacing anything. Being able to search for text in this fashion will be of particular use if you have a very large amount of text stored in your spreadsheet.

5.9 Producing graphs in a spreadsheet

Take a look at **Screen dump 5.6** to see what is to be achieved next.

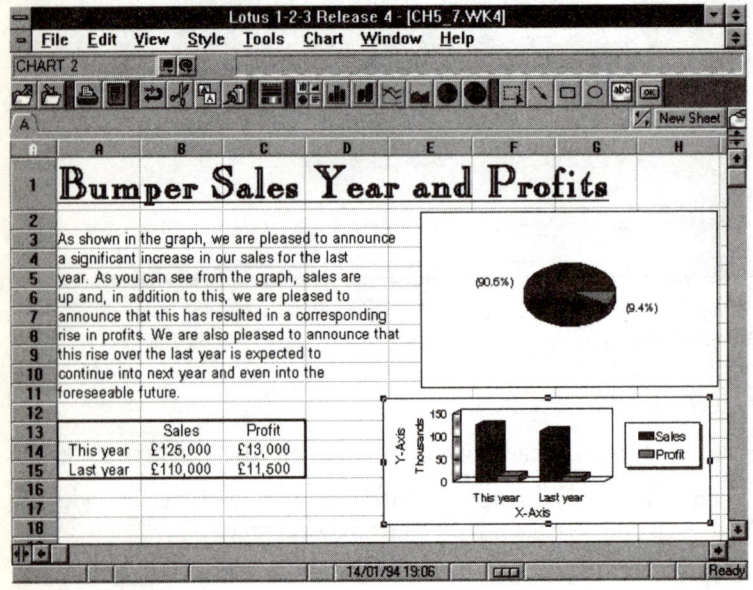

Screen dump 5.6

STYLE AND PRESENTATION

Type in the table that appears in the bottom left-hand corner.

Cell	Data
A14	This year
A15	Last year
B13	Sales
C13	Profit
B14	125,000
B15	110,000
C14	13,000
C15	11,500

- Format the four numeric values to currency, with zero decimal places. Centre data in all 9 cells.

- Highlight cells A13 to C15 and, with the Lines & Color option, give the cells a thick line border.

At this stage you have the text and table nicely boxed up.

You will produce two graphs: a pie chart showing the percentages of Sales and Profits; a bar chart showing Sales and Profit for This Year and for Last Year. Remember, you can have as many graphs/charts open at any one time as you want.

Pie Chart

- Highlight cells A14 to C15.

- Click on Tools, then Chart.

- Move the pointer to the area of the spreadsheet to the right of the text. Press down the left-hand mouse button, drag the pointer to make a box, then release the mouse button.

- Click on the 3-D Pie Chart SmartIcon.

- Click on the Title box in the graph and press the **Delete** key on your keyboard.

- With the pointer on the graph, hold down the left-hand mouse button and drag the whole graph box to another part of the screen.

Bar Chart

- Highlight cells A14 to C15.
- Click on Tools, then Chart.
- Move the pointer to the area of the spreadsheet below the Pie Chart. Press down the left-hand mouse button, drag the pointer to make a box, then release the mouse button.
- Click on the 3-D Bar Chart SmartIcon.
- Click on Chart, then Legend.
- In the Legend dialogue box click on A-This Year in the Series box, then highlight the Legend entry box.
- Move the pointer to the spreadsheet, highlight cells B13 to B15, then click on the OK button. Use **Screen dump 5.7** to check the dialogue box settings.

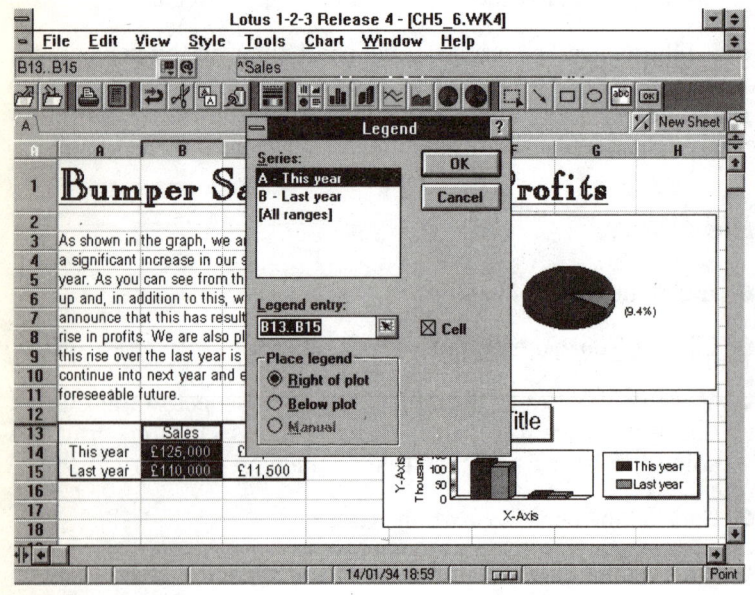

Screen dump 5.7

- Again, Click on Chart, then Legend.

- In the Legend dialogue box click on B-Last Year in the Series box, then highlight the Legend entry box.
- Move the pointer to the spreadsheet, highlight cells C13 to C15, then click on the OK button.
- Click on Chart, then Ranges.
- In the Ranges dialogue box click on X-Axis labels in the Series box, then highlight the Range entry box.
- Move the pointer to the spreadsheet, highlight cells A14 to A15, then click on the OK button.
- Again, click on Chart, then Ranges.
- In the Ranges dialogue box click on A-Sales in the Series box, then highlight the Range entry box.
- Move the pointer to the spreadsheet, highlight cells B14 to B14, then click on the OK button.
- Again, click on Chart, then Ranges.
- In the Ranges dialogue box click on B-Profit in the Series box, then highlight the Range entry box.
- Move the pointer to the spreadsheet, highlight cells C14 to C15, the click on the OK button.

Now rearrange the boxes to make an attractive printout. Save the file, and print the results.

5.10 Chapter summary

It is worth noting that spreadsheets are often set up by people experienced in this area but are operated by others who want to look at the data and carry out simple operations. Good presentation is very important if someone with limited skills in spreadsheet handling is going to extract information from them. If you return to spreadsheets you have designed after a long absence, you may be unable to find your way around if they are badly presented and muddled. Therefore, presentation and organisation, central themes of this chapter, are all important.

In this chapter you have

- altered cell widths to fit the data in them;
- named and used ranges as both a way of better documentation and a more efficient way of working with ranges;
- had more practice formatting ranges of cells;
- used the Lotus 1-2-3 date function for display and calculations;
- protected ranges of data from being over written;
- written and manipulated text boxes;
- used search and replace;
- created different kinds of graphs;
- produced attractively presented text, data and graphs.

6
DATES AND DECISIONS

6.1 Aims of this chapter

This chapter further develops the use of dates, building up formulae and moving cell contents around the spreadsheet. It also looks at Lotus 1-2-3's ability to ask questions and give results based on these questions. The chapter does this with two examples, the first trading in shares and the second a monthly sales analysis.

6.2 More practice with formats

This first example is designed to show you more about writing formulae, manipulating dates, moving ranges and inserting rows and columns.

Screen dump 6.3 is what you are aiming for (note the three parts). You will set it up in a slightly different way across the screen so that you can move things around for practice.

- Start with a blank spreadsheet and type in a company title – R Enterprises will do, but use any company name you wish.

- Next, type in identification labels. Use your mouse to speed things up.

Cell

D3	Commission Rate
A4	Purchase
A6	Date
B6	Shares
C6	Price
D6	Commission
E6	Cost

- Widen column D.

- Type in cell F3 the value: 3%. The figure 0.03 will appear in the control panel; 3% in the spreadsheet. If F3 contains 0.03, format it to Percent and to zero decimal places.

- Centre the labels in cells A6 to E6.

- Draw a line from cell A5 to cell E5. Click on Tools, then Draw, then Line. The pointer turns into a broken black cross when it is positioned on the spreadsheet. Hold down the left-hand mouse button and drag the pointer to where you want the line to end, then let go. You must draw a straight line. It's quite tricky, so practise once or twice. When the line itself is clicked on, it shows a black box either end. It can then be deleted or moved around.

- Repeat this operation for the line in cells A7 to E7.

- Click on cell A1 and enlarge and embolden the title.

At this stage you should have a spreadsheet looking similar to that in **Screen dump 6.1**.

The lines that have been drawn on rows 5 and 7 on **Screen dump 6.1** are in the form of floating objects. This means they 'float' on top of the spreadsheet and will not effect any data 'behind' them. The graphs in Chapter 3 were also floating objects that could be moved around the spreadsheet without affecting any data on it.

DATES AND DECISIONS

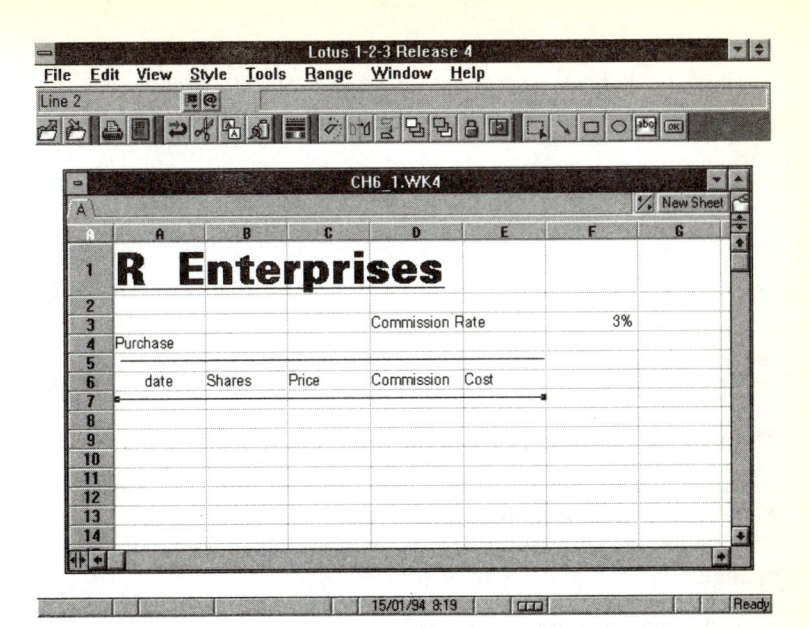

Screen dump 6.1

6.3 More on manipulating dates

Begin by typing in the purchase date, 20 October 1994. You could type in the date as a label by prefixing it with an apostrophe. However, in this exercise, you will require the computer to perform some arithmetic on this date and so the entry must be typed in as a function similar to that performed in Chapter 5.

● Click on cell A8 and type in @DATE (94, 10, 20), that is Year, Month, Day.

The figure 34627 should appear which, remember, represents the number of days since 1 January 1900. At this stage format this column as dates:

● Highlight cells A8 to A10.

● Click on Style, then Number Format.

- In the Format box in the Number Format dialogue box, highlight the 31-Dec-94 format, then click on the OK button.

Remember, Lotus 1-2-3 allows you to format cells before you type in data:

- Click on cell B8 and type in 100 – the number of shares purchased.
- Click on cell C8 and type in 0.5 (i.e. 50 pence or cents) – the share price.
- Now format the cells C8 to E10 as currency, to two decimal places.
- Click on cell D8 and type in the formula +B8*C8*$F$3.

The formula in cell D8 contains an absolute cell reference F3. Remember, when this formula is copied, all cell references with a dollar sign placed in front of them will not alter, while others will change relative to the cell they are copied to.

You will see the figure £1.50 in cell D8.

- Click on cell E8 and type in the formula +B8*C8+D8.

The formula in cell E8 multiplies the number of shares by the price per share and then adds the commission to this to give the final cost of this transaction.

- Now type in the next two rows of data:

In Cell	Type in
A9	@DATE (94, 12, 6)
B9	500
C9	1.5 [this will appear as £1.50]
A10	@DATE (93, 8, 18)
B10	150
C10	1 [this will appear as £1.00]

- Now copy the formulae in the source cells D8 to E8 to the destination cells D9 to E10.
- Save the spreadsheet with the name HST1.

Regular saving of your work at intervals is recommended. Situations do arise when you are drawn away from your computer and the system is shut down by someone else leaving all your efforts as lost. You may also experience power failures or make a silly mistake that causes your work to be lost. If you save your work every 15 minutes, for example, you need only go back 15 minutes if your spreadsheet is inadvertently lost.

Correcting mistakes

If you do make a mistake, click on the Undo SmartIcon and your last action will be 'undone'.

6.4 Copying and moving ranges

This section will deal with expanding the spreadsheet further to include details about the sale of these shares at a later date. It requires the movement of ranges. As the sales information will be similar to purchase information, it seems common sense to take advantage of this fact.

- Highlight cells A4 to E10.
- Click on Range, then Name, then name the range Purchase.

[If you are release 1 user, copy the contents of Purchase to cell F4 using Quick Copy from the pull-down menu.]

- Highlight cells A4 to E10, position the mouse pointer on the edge so the small hand shows, hold down the **Ctrl** key and the left mouse button at the same time, and drag a copy of the block of cells to start at cell F4.

This is a rather useful alternative to the Copy and Paste facilities.

Take note now of how Lotus 1-2-3 has copied the range. It assumes that F4 is the top left cell of the range copied in the same way as A4 is of the source range. In order to be consistent in naming ranges, it should be done for this next range.

- Cells F4 to J10 should still be highlighted.
- Click on Range, then Name, then name the range Sale.

For now, the entire spreadsheet will not be visible on the screen and the range Sale will be wrongly labelled. As a further demonstration of the benefits of naming ranges try the following:

- Go to cell A1 by pressing the **Home** key on the keyboard.
- Now press function key **F5**, which is the "go to" key.
- Instead of typing in a cell reference, click on SALE and then click on the OK button.

This takes you to cell F4, the top left part of the range. Next you should amend the details in this range.

- Type in a new label for cell F4: Sale; and change the label in cell J6 from Cost to Amount
- Centre the label in cell J6.
- In cell F8 type @DATE (94, 12, 28) 28 December 1994.

The correct date format (i.e. 28-Dec-94) should now appear because the range you copied from had this cell formatted for the date format.

- Click on cell G8 and type 90, the number of shares, and click on cell H8 and type 0.84, the price of shares.

The broker's commission in cell I8 has automatically been calculated for you. Observe the formula in this cell and see how the reference point to the commission rate (which is stored in cell F3) is preserved because of its absolute status in the formula. It should read +G8*H8*$F$3.

- Click on cell F3 and type in a new commission rate of 5%.

This will change the commissions in both the Purchase and Sale ranges.

- Work out a formula for cell J8 to calculate the amount received from the share sale. If you do not arrive at the figure £71.82 in the cell then read on.
- The formula is +G8*H8−I8, which is the price per share multiplied by the number sold, less the commission.
- Now type in the next two rows of data to replace the figures copied from cells A8 to B10.

In Cell Type in

F9   @DATE (94, 12, 28)
G9   300
H9   1.45
F10   @DATE (95, 01, 15)
G10   100
H10   1.4

● Now copy the formulae from cells I8 and J8 to cells I9 to J10.

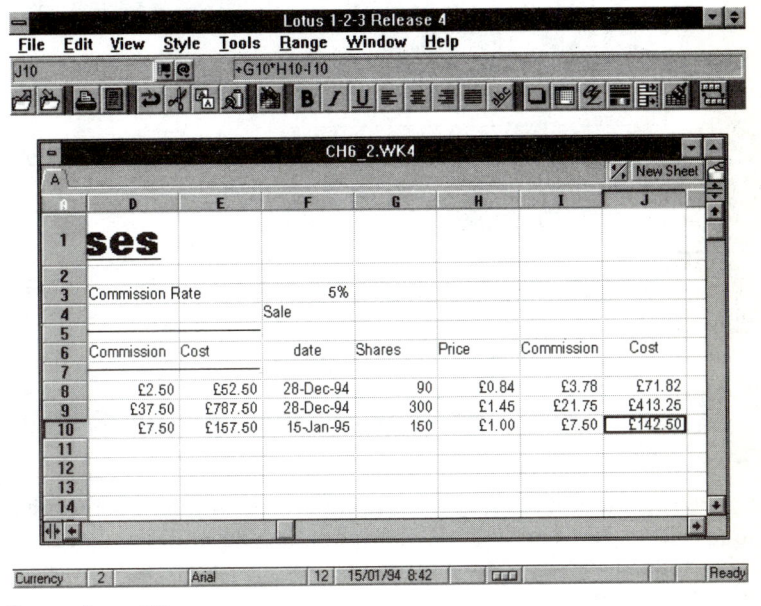

Screen dump 6.2

6.5 The @if function

You will now set up a section of the spreadsheet which will calculate the profit or loss of each share dealing and determine whether a gain is long term or short term. To be sure that you appreciate the nature of this problem, an explanation of the assumptions will first be stated.

The calculation of profit or loss is based on the difference of the final purchase price for each set of shares against the final selling

— 107 —

price. It needs to be borne in mind that not all shares are sold off; hence it is not simply a formula of amount less cost.

Screen dump 6.3 showing the entire contents of the spreadsheet is now visible.

Screen dump 6.3

The criterion for short-term or long-term gains will be whether the difference in the dates exceeds one year (365 days). If the dates are more than a year apart, then the gain or loss is long-term, otherwise it is short-term.

- Highlight cells F4 to J10 and drag the whole range to cells A12 to E18.

- Maximise the spreadsheet area.

- Type in the following labels:

    F14   Gain (Loss)
    G14   Term.

Cell F16 is going to contain the degree of gain or loss. Think carefully about how this is worked out. You will need to get Lotus 1-2-3 to calculate how much you would have paid for the shares sold before you can determine the gain or loss. This will be the purchase price for the shares plus the commission, i.e. price shares sold for less price paid for shares. Price shares sold for is the share selling price per share (cell C16) multiplied by the number sold (cell B16) less the commission. Price paid for shares is share purchase price per share (cell C8) multiplied by number sold (cell B16) plus the commission.

Think carefully about this before accepting the formula.

The formula is, therefore:

+B16*C16*(100%–$F$3) – C8*B16*(100%+$F$3)

- Type this formula into cell F16.
- Format the cell to currency and to 2 decimal places.
- Copy the formula and format in cell F16 to cells F17 to F18.

Now for the IF command that will determine whether the transaction is long-term or short-term. The logic of it goes something like this:

If the difference between the selling date and purchase date is greater than 365 then "Long" will appear in cell G16. If not, "Short" will appear.

To achieve this, click on cell G16 and type:

@IF (A16–A8>365, "Long", "Short").

The @IF statement appears in brackets and is broken into three components.

The first part is the argument. In this case it is A16–A8>365, which calculates the value of cell A16 less the value of cell A8 (which are dates in number form) and determines if it is greater than 365.

The second part appears after the first comma and is an instruction as to what should be done if the argument is true. In this instance, it is to place the word Long in the cell.

The third part that appears after the second comma is an instruction as to what should be done if the argument is false. In this instance, it is to place the word Short in the cell.

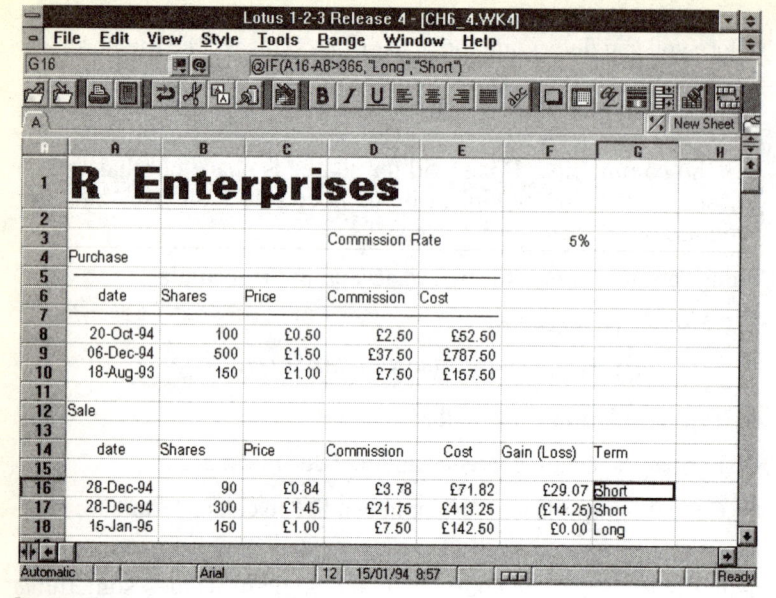

Screen dump 6.4

- Copy this formula from cell G16 to cells G17 to G18.
- Examine **Screen dump 6.4** to give you an idea of what you should have achieved by now.

The last two entries made into you spreadsheet are complex, and you may need time to ponder over them. Experiment for a while by:

Altering the commission rate
Altering the dates
Altering the purchase and selling price of the shares.

- Save your spreadsheet as HST2 before moving on to the next section.
- Print out the spreadsheet, remembering to define the range to be printed.
- Click on File, then Close to put away your spreadsheet in preparation for the next one.

6.6 Relative and absolute formulae

The next example uses a list of dates and numbers of caravans sold by a particular dealer over a particular year. See **Screen dump 6.5**. This example will give you further practice developing formulae and achieving good presentation.

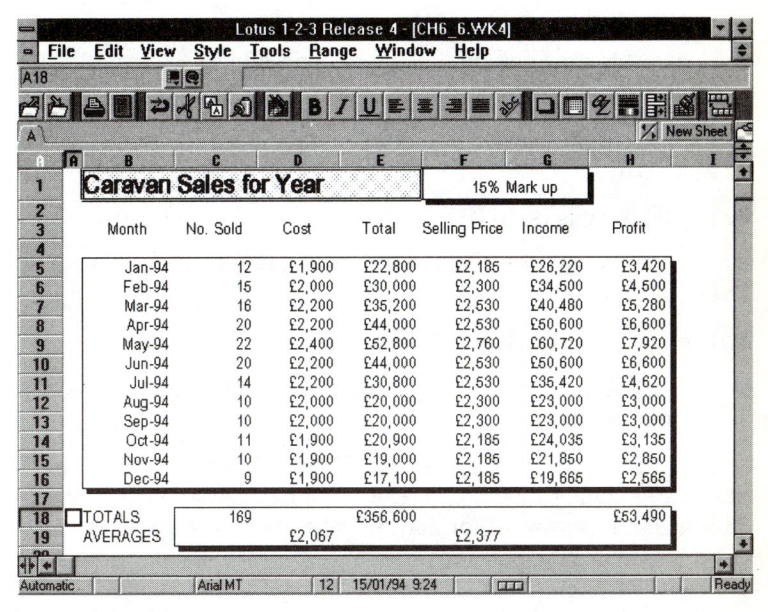

	B	C	D	E	F	G	H
1	Caravan Sales for Year				15% Mark up		
3	Month	No. Sold	Cost	Total	Selling Price	Income	Profit
5	Jan-94	12	£1,900	£22,800	£2,185	£26,220	£3,420
6	Feb-94	15	£2,000	£30,000	£2,300	£34,500	£4,500
7	Mar-94	16	£2,200	£35,200	£2,530	£40,480	£5,280
8	Apr-94	20	£2,200	£44,000	£2,530	£50,600	£6,600
9	May-94	22	£2,400	£52,800	£2,760	£60,720	£7,920
10	Jun-94	20	£2,200	£44,000	£2,530	£50,600	£6,600
11	Jul-94	14	£2,200	£30,800	£2,530	£35,420	£4,620
12	Aug-94	10	£2,000	£20,000	£2,300	£23,000	£3,000
13	Sep-94	10	£2,000	£20,000	£2,300	£23,000	£3,000
14	Oct-94	11	£1,900	£20,900	£2,185	£24,035	£3,135
15	Nov-94	10	£1,900	£19,000	£2,185	£21,850	£2,850
16	Dec-94	9	£1,900	£17,100	£2,185	£19,665	£2,565
18	TOTALS	169		£356,600			£53,490
19	AVERAGES		£2,067		£2,377		

Screen dump 6.5

Each month a number of caravans are sold (e.g. 10 in August). They cost £2,000 each, which is a total cost of £20,000. The 15% mark-up gives a selling price of £2,300 per caravan. The profit is worked out as the difference between selling price and cost price multiplied by the number sold.

- Type the title Caravan Sales for Year in cell A1, then change (to taste) Font & Attributes (click on Style, then Font & Attributes).

- Highlight cells A1 to D1, then give the range some lines, borders and colours in order to make the appearance more attractive (click on Style, then Lines & Color).

- The column headings with cell locations are:

Cell	Type in
A3	Month
B3	No. Sold
C3	Cost
D3	Total
E3	Selling Price
F3	Income
G3	Profit

- Centre align the column headings (highlight the range A3 to G3, then click on the centre SmartIcon).

- Type in all the numbers sold in column B for the range of cells B5 to B16.

- Highlight cells B5 to B16.

- Click on Range, then Name, and type in SOLD, then click on the OK button.

- In cell F1 type the label Mark up.

- In cell E1 type 15%. Now format cell E1 to Percent, to zero decimal places.

Next you will type in a date in cell A5 and get the program to calculate the remaining months. In order to appreciate the usefulness of this facility, it is wise to format the cells where the dates are to be typed before putting dates into them.

- Highlight cells A5 to A16.

- Click on Number Format, then highlight Dec-93, then click the OK button. [Range pull-down menu for Release 1]. The cells will stay empty, but they have been formatted to all present dates the same way.

- In cell A5 type in the date using the @DATE function: @DATE (94, 1, 1).

- Now click on cell A6 and type in the formula +A5+31.

The purpose of this is to add 31 days to January 1st to go into February.

- Now copy the formula in cell A6 to the destination range A7 to A16.

Each consecutive month should appear from January to December. Each cell containing this formula is derived by being 31 higher than the cell above.

- At this stage, browse through the cells and examine each formula in the range A5 to A16 and be clear in your own mind about what has happened.

The concept of such formulae copying always taking a relative set of values is an important one. Look again to see how the concept works.

- Type the Cost figures into column C, using **Screen dump 6.5**.

- Click on cell D5 and type in a formula that will calculate the total cost of the caravans to the trader: +C5*B5.

- Now copy the formula in cell D5 to the destination range D6 to D16.

- Highlight and Name the range D5 to D16 as COSTS.

Again, observe what has happened in the cells in this range. Each formula is a multiple of the cell two positions to the left and one to the left.

Now you will see where this principle is not what is wanted in determining the selling price. The formula you want in cell E5 is one that multiplies the cost in cell C5 by the percentage mark-up set up in cell E1 added to the original cost. In fact, the formula will be: (C5*E1)+C5. Note that the use of brackets ensures the multiplication is done before adding the original figure.

- Click on cell E5 and type in this formula.

- Now use the copy command to copy the formula in cell E5 to the destination range E6 to E16.

Something is wrong!

Observe the formula in this range of cells and you will see that the percentage to work with is always assumed to be four cells directly above. In fact, although this relative position has worked in your favour up until now, you want to **fix** the cell E1 in the formula. Define an absolute cell value by placing a $ (dollar) sign in front of the cell location; in other words, instead of placing E1 in the formula place $E$1.

- Click on cell E5 and amend the formula to: (C5*$E$1)+C5.

- Now copy the formula in cell E5 to the destination range E6 to E16.

You should now have the desired result.

On a technical note, only the second part (the row number) needed to be fixed, as the column E bit would have stayed correct. Lotus allows you to mix the absolute with relative references in a formula. In other words E$1 would have worked as well, making the formula (C5*E$1)+C5.

- Click on cell F5 and type in the formula +E5*B5, then copy this formula to the range F6 to F16. This multiplies the selling price by the number sold to give the total income.

- To complete the spreadsheet click on cell G5 and type in the formula +F5−D5, then copy this formula to the range G6 to G16. This subtracts total cost from total income to give the profit.

- Highlight and Name the range G5 to G16 as PROFIT.
- Click on cell A18 and type in the label: TOTALS.
- Click on cell B18 and type in the function:@SUM (SOLD).
- Click on cell D18 and type in the function: @SUM (COSTS).
- Click on cell G18 and type in the function: @SUM (PROFIT).
- Click on cell A20 and type in the label AVERAGES.
- Highlight and Name the range C5 to C16 as COST.
- Click on cell A19 and type in the label: AVERAGES.
- Click on cell C19 and type in the function: @AVG (COST).
- Highlight and Name the range E5 to E16 as SELLING.
- Click on cell E19 and type in the function: @AVG (SELLING).

In order to tidy up your spreadsheet, do the following:

- Remove the grid lines (click on View, then Set View Preferences, then click on Grid lines, then OK.
- Format all money figures to currency, with zero decimal places.
- Right align cells A5 to A16.
- Highlight cells A5 to G16, and give them a border.

- Give a border and colour for the ranges: E1 to F1; A18 to G19.

The spreadsheet is tighter against the left edge than it needs to be, so move it one column to the right.

- Save your spreadsheet for possible future reference and practice.

6.7 Chapter summary

In this chapter you have:

- manipulated text around the spreadsheet;
- formatted ranged with dates and currencies;
- entered dates and further manipulated them using the @DATE function;
- copied relative and absolute formulae;
- moved ranges around a spreadsheet by either cut and paste or dragging a range to a new location;
- had more practice using named ranges to build formulae.

7
LOTUS 1-2-3 DATABASE

7.1 Aims of this chapter

This chapter examines the way Lotus 1-2-3 allows you to set up tables of data and then rearrange them into a different logical order. In doing so, it also examines a method whereby a table can be rearranged by a single operation from the keyboard rather then performing a whole string of command entries through the Lotus 1-2-3 menus.

It is often useful to be able to extract specific information from a data table – for example, unsold houses in a list of property details held by an estate agent. This example is developed in the latter part of this chapter.

7.2 Setting out a database table

Screen dump 7.1 will show you what you are trying to achieve in this chapter.

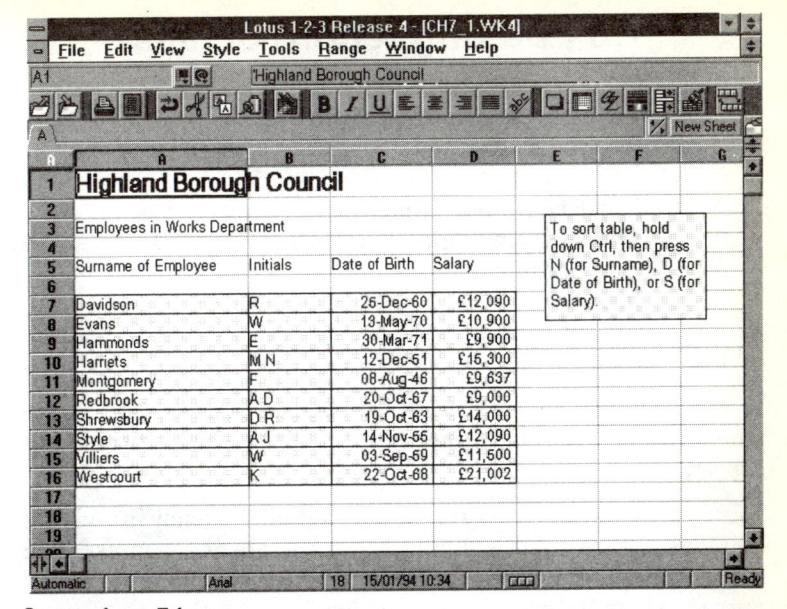

Screen dump 7.1

Here we will learn how to set up the program to rearrange the information: Surname, Data of Birth, Salary in ascending or descending order, as required.

When lists are exceptionally long, this facility is extremely useful. Also, if a single employee has to be added to the list, then you need only insert a new line on the spreadsheet, enter the details and use the **Ctrl** key command to rearrange the information back into sorted order. Before starting it is worth making yourself familiar with some of the jargon that this chapter will introduce you to.

A database can be defined as a collection of pieces of information organised in a meaningful way. Consider a phone directory, which lists names, addresses, and phone numbers. In the phone book, these data are arranged in a table of three columns. Each entry in the phone book is thus divided into three parts: name, address, phone number. In technical terms, each entry in the phone book is called a "record"; each section into which each record is divided is called a "field". Once you have grasped these concepts, you are well on your way to understanding what databases are all about.

7.3 Entering record details

- Start by typing in the required header labels:

Cell	Label
A1	Highland Borough Council
A3	Employees in Works Department
A5	Surname of Employee
B5	Initials
C5	Date of Birth
D5	Salary

At this point you will need to widen columns A and C so that the labels can be seen. Give the title in cell A1 a more prominent appearance.

Next you will need to type in the details of each individual employee. Each row (or line) on the spreadsheet represents a record of an employee with the cell locations holding fields: Surname, Initials, Date of Birth, and Salary.

- Type in the record details from **Screen dump 7.1**, remembering that dates will have to be entered in function form @DATE (year, month, day). Then you will have to format the date (Style, Number Format, 31-Dec-93).

- Format the salary figures to currency and to zero decimal places.

You want to add a text box. Click on Tools, then Draw, then Text.

- Position the dotted cross that appears on E3 and click.

Type in: To sort table, hold down Ctrl, then press either N (for Surname), D (for Date of Birth), or S (for Salary). Hold down the left mouse button and drag the box to anywhere on the sheet is best. To edit the text double click on the box. To alter the appearance of the text object, right click on it and select the required options.

In the database you must ensure that:

1. Each column contains one **field**.

2. Each field name is unique i.e. does not appear twice.

3. Each **record** is kept on one row.

LOTUS 1–2–3 DATABASE

7.4 Sorting the records

Before beginning with the sort, you should NAME certain parts of your spreadsheet in order to conform to better spreadsheet practice and to get a better "feel" for the concept of database.

- Highlight cells A7 to D16. Name this range DATABASE.
- Now repeat this for each **field** range, column by column

Block	Name
A7..A16	SURNAME
B7..B16	INITIALS
C7..C16	DATE OF BIRTH
D7..D16	SALARY

The next task is to rearrange the records into surname order.

- Click on Range, then Sort.

Now you need to define the database range and how you want it sorted.

- In the Range box in the Sort dialogue box, type DATABASE.

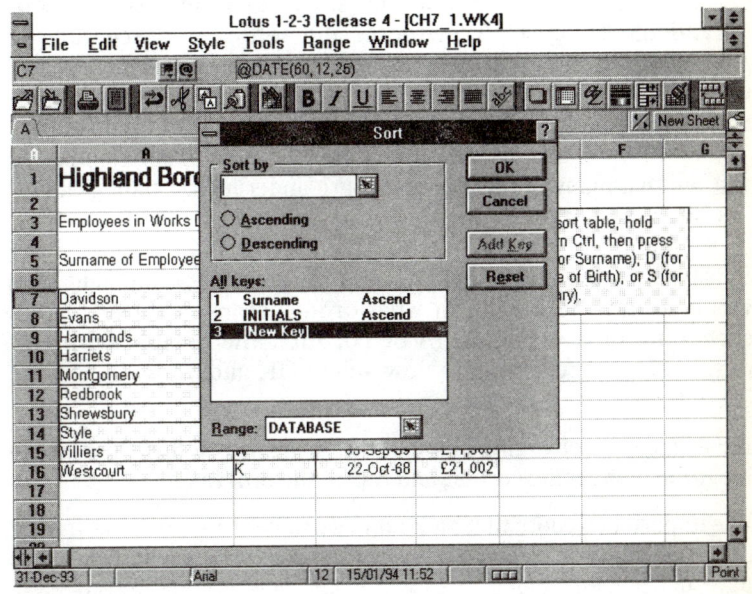

Screen dump 7.2

[At this stage Release 1 users should go to the next Section.]

Having defined where the database range is, the next stage is to indicate what field you want to sort.

- In the Sort by box in the Sort dialogue box, type SURNAME.
- The default setting should be Ascending (determining how the records are sorted alphabetically).
- Click on the Add Key button.

In the event that you have more than one of the same surnames you will want to sort the initials.

- In the Sort by box type INITIALS.
- Click on the Add Key to see the second sort key added to the All keys box.
- Now click on the OK button and you will see the effect.

[Data Sort with Release 1: Having defined where the database range is, the next stage is to indicate what field you want to sort the records by, i.e. the Primary key field. Enter SURNAME as the range that contains the primary key field. You will also have to decide in what order you want the records to appear, ascending or descending (A or D). Alter the default setting of descending to Ascending. In the event that two surnames are the same, you will want to decide on what basis to sort the common records. This is when you need to define a Secondary key. Now go to the Primary section of the dialogue box. If you observe your dialogue box you will see that many of the characters are underlined. Holding the Alt key and pressing one of these keys to get there has the same effect as highlighting the option with your mouse and clicking. Enter INITIALS as the range that contains the secondary key field. You will also have to decide in what order you want these sorted, ascending or descending (A or D). Alter the default setting of descending to Ascending. Now select OK and you will see the effect.]

Experiment by changing some of the surnames so that they are no longer in alphabetical order, and repeat the process.

It is important to note that data ranges can be sorted without having to name ranges in the way you have throughout this chapter. If you have not named ranges, then you would need to type in range co-ordinates rather than range names.

7.5 Sorting using macros

In many circumstances, you want to replace a sequence of commands with just one key stroke.

You will record the sorting procedure in a format called a **macro**. A macro simply performs a number of keystrokes for you. You will start the macro with the press of one key (or, in this case, holding down the **Ctrl** key and pressing one key).

- Click on Tools, then Macro, then Record. (Everything you now do will be recorded until you tell the computer to stop recording.) You will now carry out the sorting procedure you have just learnt.

- Click on Range, then Sort.

- Click on Reset.

- In the Range box in the Sort dialogue box, type DATABASE.

- In the Sort by box, type SURNAME.

- Click on the Add Key button.

- In the Sort by box, type INITIALS.

- Click on the Add Key button, then on the OK button.

The rows will have sorted into ascending alphabetical order.

- Click on Tools, then Macro, then Stop Recording.

- Click again on Tools, then Macro, then Show Transcript.

A Transcript window will appear in the lower left-hand corner of the screen. This is a transcript of what you have just done. See **Screen dump 7.3**.

As you perform your commands, the Lotus 1-2-3 program is creating the sequence of commands that it uses to perform the actions. By recording commands in this way, you are effectively getting Lotus to write a program for you. This will form the basis of your Macro.

You can increase the size of the transcript window by either clicking on its maximise button or stretching it wider with your mouse.

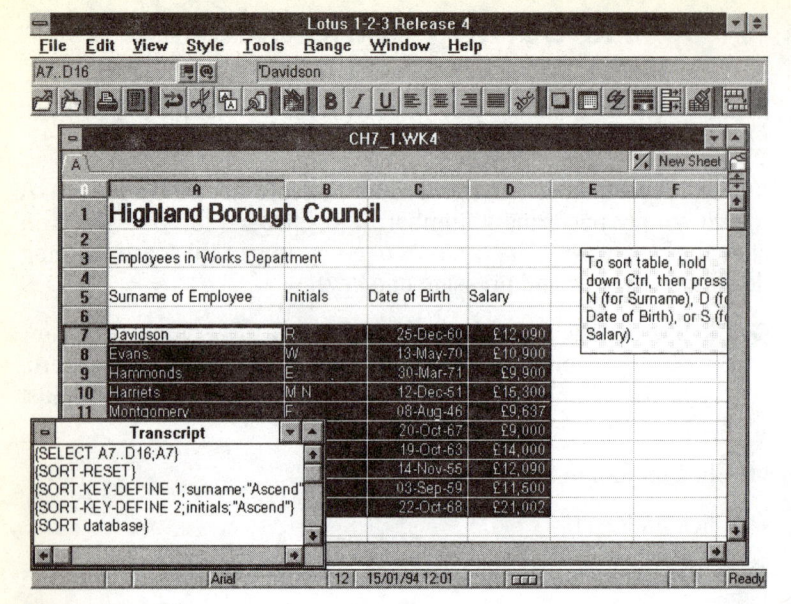

Screen dump 7.3

- Highlight and copy to the clipboard the entire contents of the Transcript box. You must use <u>C</u>ut from the Edit menu to do this.

- Click back in the spreadsheet. The Transcript box will disappear. Click on cell A18 and paste the transcript.

- Click on <u>T</u>ools, then <u>M</u>acro, then Hide Tra<u>n</u>script.

You will now assign the macro, which should be pasted into cells A18 to A22, as a Range Name which can be called up with one Key stroke.

- Click on <u>R</u>ange, then <u>N</u>ame.

- In the <u>R</u>ange box in the Name dialogue box, type in A18 .. A22.

- Click on the <u>N</u>ame box and type in \N.

- Then click on the OK button.

- Alter the surname Davidson to Williams.

Hold down the **Ctrl** key and press N: the records will now sort into alphabetical order by surname and initial.

Repeat these instructions for Date of Birth (\D) and Salary (\S). In the Sort dialogue box click on Reset, first of all. The respective transcripts will be as shown in **Screen dump 7.4**.

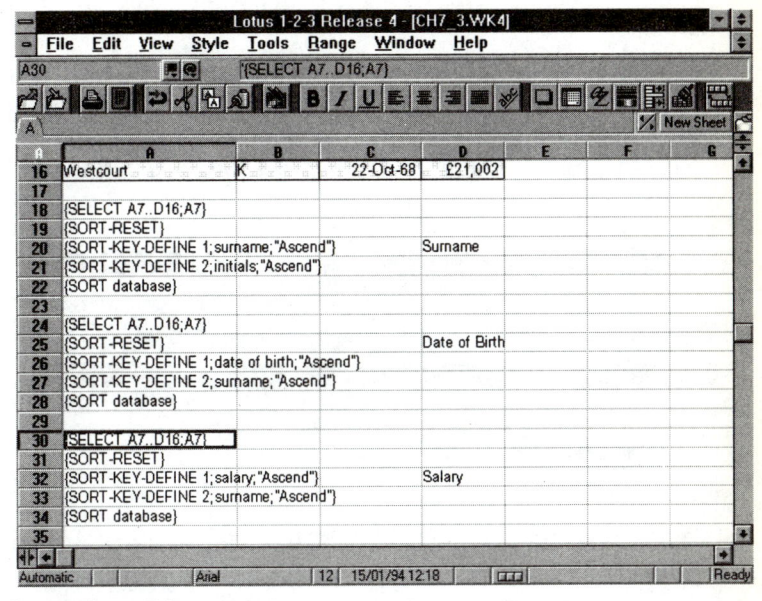

Screen dump 7.4

(Note: The macros *must* stay in the spreadsheet. They can, however, be moved well out of the way by highlighting all the cells as dragging the highlighted cells to a new location.)

Change names, dates of birth and salaries to see these keys work.

Macro buttons

As well as assign a macro to a key stroke, you can create a button on the screen which, when pressed, carries out the function as shown in **Screen dump 7.5**.

- Click on the text box at E3 and then press the Del or Delete key.
- Click on Tools, then Draw, then Button. The pointer becomes a black cross. Hold down the left mouse button and drag the cross to form an elongated button. Let go of the mouse button.

- In the Assign to Button dialogue box, click on the arrow in the Assign macro from: box. Highlight **Range**. Click on the Button text: box, delete Button, and type in Sort by Surname. Highlight \S in the Existing named ranges box, and then click the OK button.

Drag the button to where you want it, then repeat for Date of Birth and Salary. Clicking on the new button performs the macro. If you click on the button with the right button you can resize the button, drag it to another location, change the label and its font, etc.

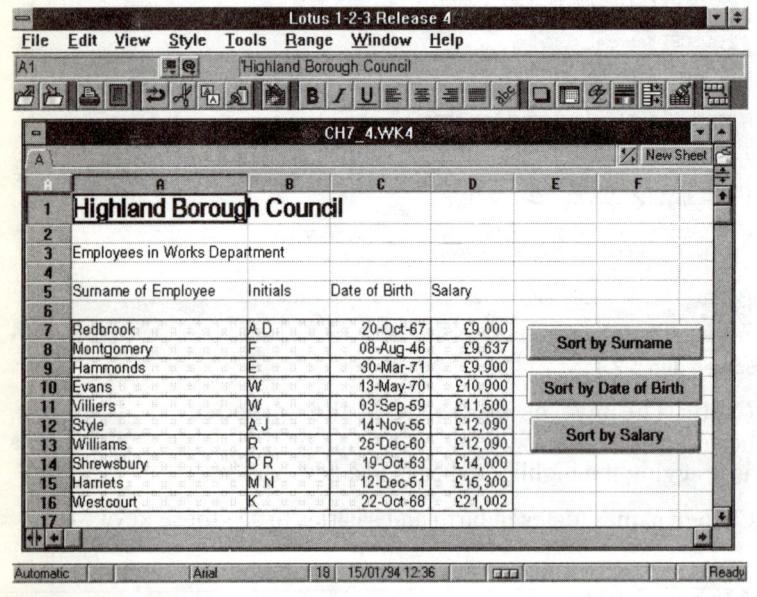

Screen dump 7.5

7.6 Enquiring and extracting information from a database

In this part of the chapter, you will use the Data Query part of the program to extract certain specified items from a list. Examine **Screen dump 7.6**.

LOTUS 1–2–3 DATABASE

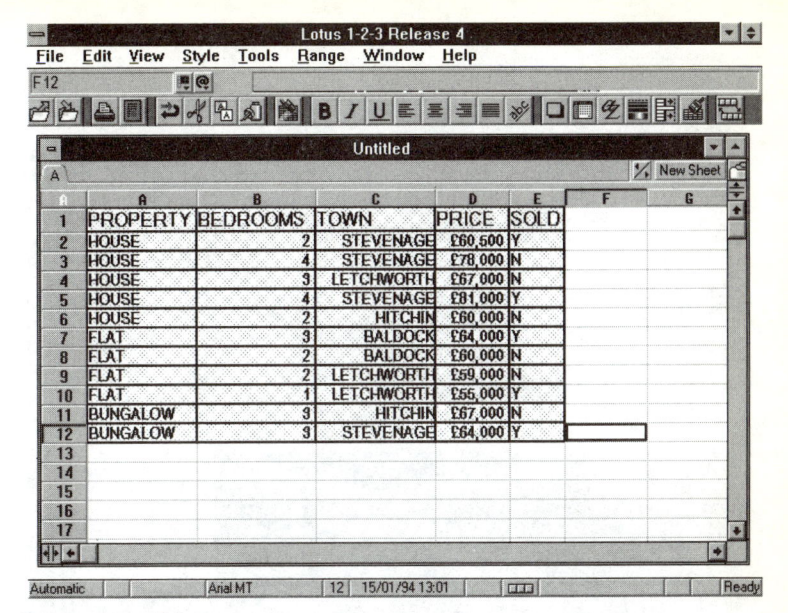

Screen dump 7.6

	A	B	C	D	E
1	PROPERTY	BEDROOMS	TOWN	PRICE	SOLD
2	HOUSE	2	STEVENAGE	£60,500	Y
3	HOUSE	4	STEVENAGE	£78,000	N
4	HOUSE	3	LETCHWORTH	£67,000	N
5	HOUSE	4	STEVENAGE	£81,000	Y
6	HOUSE	2	HITCHIN	£60,000	N
7	FLAT	3	BALDOCK	£64,000	Y
8	FLAT	2	BALDOCK	£60,000	N
9	FLAT	2	LETCHWORTH	£59,000	N
10	FLAT	1	LETCHWORTH	£55,000	Y
11	BUNGALOW	3	HITCHIN	£67,000	N
12	BUNGALOW	3	STEVENAGE	£64,000	Y

The aim is quite simple: to extract from the table a list of all those houses that have not been sold. Start by acquainting yourself with some more jargon. What you do is set up a query table on to which you will copy all the required data. The criteria section will represent the table from which you want to select the data.

● Begin by typing in all the details into a new spreadsheet. You will need to widen some columns.

In **Screen dump 7.6** the Alignment option from the Style pull-down menu was used to justify the town names in column C to the right of their cells. Also, the prices are displayed in £s. The table has also been given a frame.

At this stage the database range is the area from cell A1 to cell E17. Each row (house details) represents a single record in the database, while each cell in a row represents a field. You have 11 records from row 2 to row 12, and each record has five fields: column A to column F. This is a simple principle well worth getting used to. At the top of each column is the field name, which will have an important part to play in the demonstration.

[If you are a Release 1 user, go the second part of this section.]

- Click on Tools, then Database, then New Query.

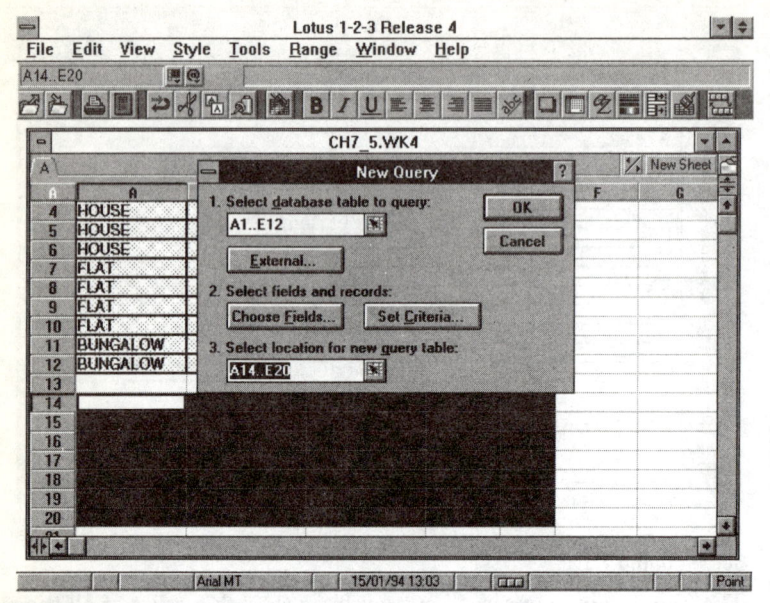

Screen dump 7.7

Screen dump 7.7 shows the resulting dialogue box with various settings for the database Table and the location for new query Table. The database Table range comprises the cells where the computer is going to look for the records. Here it is A1..E12. It is important to note that the database Table *must* include the field names at the top of the column. This is different from the database Range used earlier in this chapter to sort data, which excluded the field names. Click on box 1: Select database table to query: and type in A1..E12.

Click on box 3: Select location for the new query table and type in A14..E30, directly underneath the database table. You can place the new query table anywhere on the spreadsheet, but if you position it underneath the database table, the column-widths are already set up correctly to suit the data, although there is no absolute need for this.

The next stage is to enter details about criteria. This is what the program needs to determine what you want selected from the database table. In this example you will work on the basis of selecting details of all unsold houses.

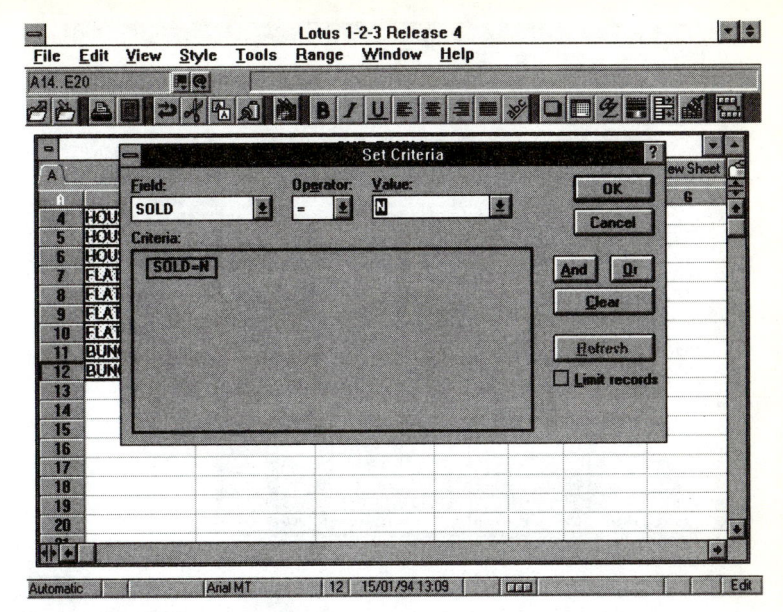

Screen dump 7.8

- Click on the Set Criteria button in box 2.

In the Set Criteria dialogue box click on the Field arrow button. All the fields in the highlighted database will be listed: Property; Bedrooms; Town; Price; Sold. Click on Sold. Move to the Value box and click on the arrow button. The fields Y N will appear. Click on N, then click on the OK button. You will return to the New Query dialogue box.

The criteria have been set so that where SOLD=N in the database table, the record will be copied to the query table. The dialogue box in **Screen dump 7.9** illustrates how this has been set up.

Click on the OK button.

You should now have the results shown in **Screen dump 7.9**.

LOTUS 1-2-3 WINDOWS

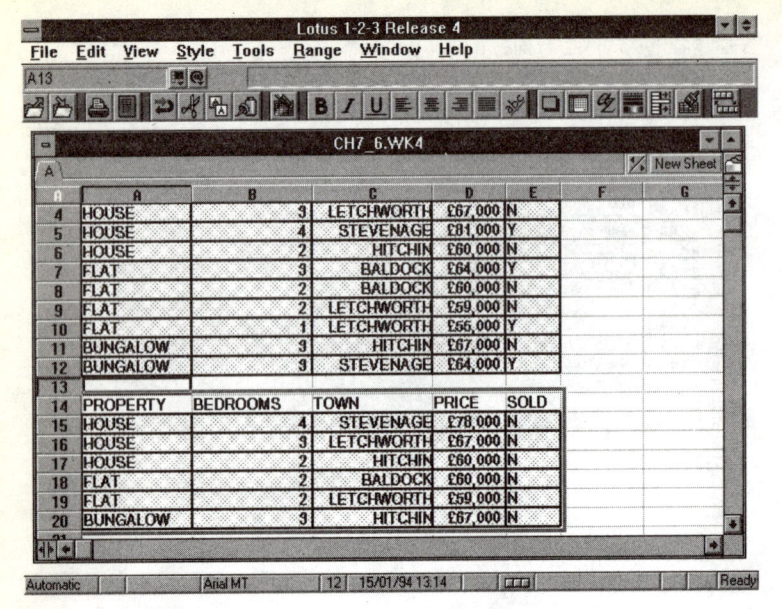

Screen dump 7.9

Now try the following:

- Click on Tools, then Database, then New query.

Set up the following parameters:

    database table (box 1)   A1..E12
    new query table (box 3)   A22..E33

    set Criteria   Price > £64,000

- Click on the OK button, then on the OK button again.

This extracts all houses with a price greater than £64,000.

Now try the following:

- Set up the following parameters:

    database table (box 1)   A1..E12
    new query table (box 3)   A28..E33

    set Criteria   Price > £60,000
                              AND
                              Price < £75,000

For this you need to create two lines of criteria. After the first one has been entered, click on the **And** button in the set criteria dialogue box.

This selects those houses whose price is greater than £60,000 AND less than £75,000 – a common type of request from a database needed in such circumstances.

Next, you will see how two criteria can be set up.

- Set up the following parameters:

    database table (box 1)   A1..E12
    new query table (box 3) A35..E44

    set Criteria   Property = House
                             AND
                             Bedrooms > 2

This extracts those properties which are houses with more than two bedrooms.

In practice, such databases may run into many hundreds of records and such facilities can prove very useful. It should also be noted that the query table can be placed onto another sheet rather than below a database table on an existing sheet. Once you have grasped the basics of performing such query analysis, setting up more sophisticated spreadsheets will not prove such a difficult step.

The final part of this section looks at deleting and finding various records in a database. Before going any further, it would be wise to save your spreadsheet in case you ever want to refer back to it. Before deleting records, it is often a good idea to save the current version of the spreadsheet in case it is needed again.

- Click on **T**ools, then Data**b**ase, then **D**elete Records.

Screen dump 7.10

If you observe **Screen dump 7.10** you will see the Delete Records dialogue box. Again, the database table has to be defined as A1..E12. Other boxes require criteria in the same way as you used before. In this example the criteria have been set so that the Field where Sold = Y will be deleted.

- Type in the database table range and the criteria as in **Screen dump 7.10**.

- Click on OK and observe the results.

The Find Records option in the Tools, Database menu works in exactly the same way as the Delete Records option except nothing is deleted – the records that meet the criteria in the database table are all highlighted.

- Restore your last spreadsheet, before you deleted the houses that are sold, by clicking on File, then Open.

- Click on Tools, then Database, then Find Records.

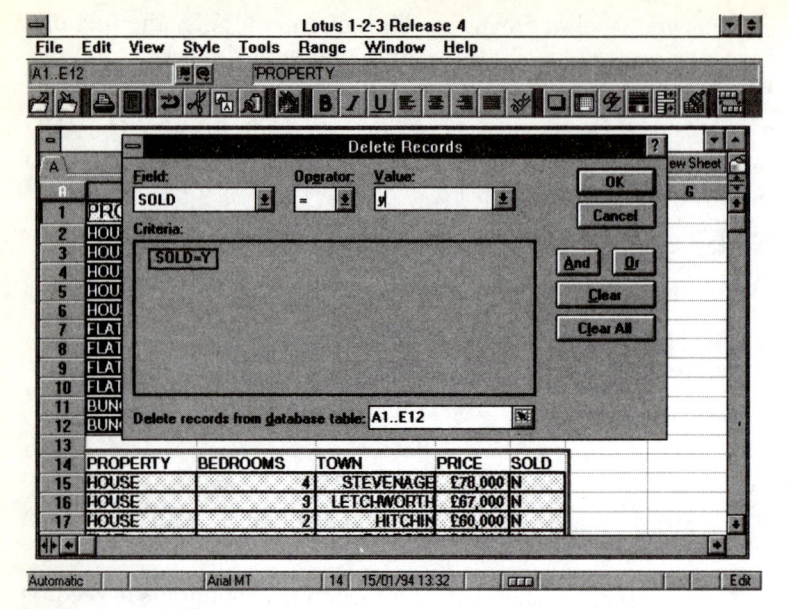

- Define the database table as A1..E12 and set the criteria as:

Field	Operator	Value
Town	=	Stevenage
AND		
Property	=	House

- Click on the OK button.

Three records in the database table will be highlighted.

[Database Enquiries and extraction with Release 1

The INPUT range is the database itself where the computer is going to look for the records. It will be the range A1..E12. It is important to note that the Input-Range must include the field names at the top of the column. This is different from the Database-Range used earlier in this chapter to sort data, as it excluded the field names.

The first stage is to enter details about a Criteria-Range. This is what the program needs to determine what you want selected from the Input-range of the database. In the example you will work on the basis of selecting details of all unsold houses.

The criteria-range is the range G1..G2. You will first need to type in data for this.

- Set up the Criteria-Range by entering into the respective cells the following details:

Cell	Label
G1	SOLD
G2	N

You use this to tell you that what you are interested in, being those records where the field name 'SOLD' has an 'N' entered. What you must now do is to tell Lotus 1-2-3 where this Criterion-Range is; in other words, give the computer a reference point. It is important that the Criterion-Range includes the field name that appears at the top of the column where the data is held.

The next stage is to decide where to put records you select. This is called the Output-Range.

- Type in the following details in their respective cells:

Cell	Location Label
A20	PROPERTY
B20	BEDROOMS
C20	TOWN
D20	PRICE
E20	SOLD

When defining the Output-Range it is important to give plenty of rows below the field headings so that there is room for the house records that match the criterion defined. You can place the Output-Range anywhere on the spreadsheet, but if you position it underneath the database query range, the column-widths are already set up correctly to suit the data, although there is no absolute need for this.

You will also observe that the Output-Range needs the field names at the top. Each field name must match one in the database query range, but does not have to be in the same order or have every field defined.

- From the Data pull-down menu, select the Query option. The dialogue box that appears needs the following range co-ordinates:

Input-range	A1..E12
Criteria-range	G1..G2
Output-range	A20..E40

- Now select the Extract option from the dialogue box.

- Go to cell A20 and inspect the results.

By doing this you should now have the results in the range starting at cell A20.

Now try the following:

- Redefine your criterion range as:

Cell	Label
G1	PRICE
G2	(D3<64000)

- From the Query option in the Data pull-down menu select the Extract option again. (The earlier range settings will not have altered.)

This has the effect of extracting all houses with a price of less than £64,000. When placing this formula into the cell you will see that a zero will be placed into the cell. This indicates that the condition is false; in other words, the zero (0) reveals that the cell value is NOT less than 64,000. When you extract from this, the operation knows that it needs to perform this throughout the database query range.

Now try the following:

- Rewrite your criterion range as:

    Cell   Label

    G1   PRICE
    G2   (D3>60000#AND#D3<75000)

- From the Query option in the Data pull-down menu select the Extract option from the dialogue box.

This indicates that the condition must be to select those houses whose price is greater than £60,000 AND less then £75,000 – a common type of request from a database needed in such circumstances.

Next, you will see how two criteria can be set up.

- Redefine your criterion range as:

    Cell   Label

    G1   PROPERTY
    G2   HOUSE
    H1   BEDROOMS
    H2   (B3>2)

- From the Query option in the Data pull-down menu, reset the Criteria-Range as being G1..H2.

- From this dialogue box select the Extract option.

The effect should be to extract those properties which are houses with more than two bedrooms and place them all in the Output range.

Before going any further, it would be wise to save your spreadsheet in case you ever want to refer back to it. Before deleting records, it is often a good idea to save the current version of the spreadsheet in case it is needed again.

- Reset your Criteria section to:

    Cell   Label

    G1   SOLD
    G2   Y

- Select Extract from the Database Query menu to place into the Output table a copy of those fields whose houses have been sold.

- Now go back to the spreadsheet and replace cell G2 with 'N'.

- From the Database Query menu select Delete.

- As a precaution, you will be asked whether you want to cancel the request or go ahead and delete it. Select Delete.

This will have the effect of deleting from the Input range all records that match the Criteria-Range. In other words, it will remove all records that have 'N' in the SOLD field.

When you delete there is no going back other than reverting back to a spreadsheet file you saved. You will see that all the records with 'N' in the SOLD field appear in the output table while all records with 'Y' in the SOLD field appear in the input table.

The Data Query Modify options allows four other options of Extract, Replace, Insert and Finish. Up until now, you will have carried out work on the input range and placed results to the output range or deleted records from the input range. The modify option is really the reverse of this in that it is concerned with placing data back from the Output Range and into the Input Range.

- From the Data pull-down menu select Query and then Modify.

- Now select the help screen associated with this by pressing the function key F1.

The help page that comes with this will give you further details about how the Data Query Modify option works.

- Go back to the Modify dialogue box and select the INSERT option to see the effect it has on the Input Range.

Finally, there are two other Data Query options:

FIND allows you to search through the Input Range to find a record that matches the conditions of the Criterion Range. RESET will reset the Input, Criterion and Output Ranges in the Query dialogue box.]

7.7 Further work with a database

In this third example you will set up a simple stock database, from it sort the records into value or stock reference order, and print a list using a macro.

To get yourself started examine **Screen dump 7.11** to see what kind of layout is required and the cell entries you want, observing the following points before you type in values, formulae and formats.

	A	B	C	D	E	F
1	Stock Records					
2						
3	Stock	Quantity	Unit	Minimum	Reorder	Stock
4	Reference		Cost	Level	Quantity	Value
5						
6	C777	12	£0.56	50	30	£6.72
7	A100	20	£1.89	10	8	£37.80
8	A224	15	£2.80	12	10	£42.00
9	A321	15	£2.99	35	20	£44.85
10	D100	31	£1.62	40	20	£50.22
11	D220	40	£3.33	30	15	£133.20
12	B109	15	£9.00	10	5	£135.00
13	A343	28	£10.00	20	10	£280.00
14	B767	23	£12.88	20	10	£296.24
15	B200	8	£55.00	10	10	£440.00
16	B652	99	£7.01	30	20	£693.99
17						
18						2160.02
19						

Screen dump 7.11

- The field Stock Reference contains labels.
- The fields Quantity, Unit Cost, Minimum Level, and Reorder Quantity are numeric entries.
- The Stock Value field is formulae entries:

  Quantity multiplied by Unit Cost. (Both formatted for currency to 2 decimal places.)
- Cell F18 is a @SUM function summing all Stock Values.
- The following ranges are NAMED. (Click on Range, then Name.)

Block	Name
A6..F16	Stock Data
A6..A16	Reference
B6..B16	Quantity
C6..C16	Unit Cost
D6..D16	Minimum Level
E6..E16	Reord. Quantity
F6..F16	Stock Value

7.8 Tracing commands for macros

In this final section you will write a macro to sort the table by value.

- Click on Tools, then Macro, then Record.
- Click on Range [Data in Release 1], then Sort.
- In the Sort dialogue box, click on the Range box and type in the range name: STOCK DATA.
- In the Sort by box, type in the range name: STOCK VALUE, click on Descending, then click on the OK button.

The spreadsheet will be highlighted and reordered according to Stock Value, with the highest value in the top line.

- Click on Tools, then Macro, then Stop Recording.

LOTUS 1-2-3 DATABASE

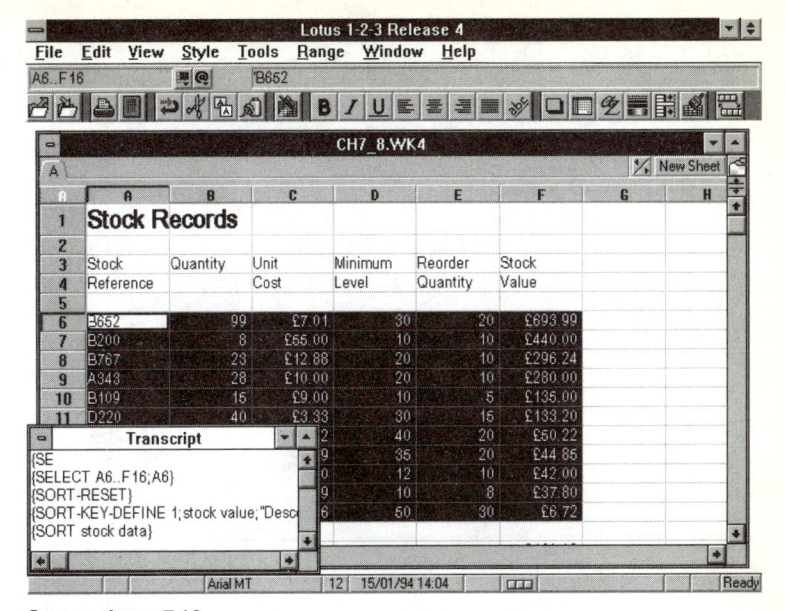

Screen dump 7.12

- Click on Tools, then Macro, then Show Transcript.

- Highlight the entire transcript and copy it. (With the mouse pointer on the highlighted area, click the right-hand mouse button, then click on Copy.)

- Move the pointer to the spreadsheet, click on cell A18 and paste the transcript.

- Highlight the cells containing the transcript (A18..A21), then click on Range, then Name. In the Name dialogue box, click on the Name box and type in \S. Click on the Add button, then on the OK button.

Now, if you hold down the **Ctrl** key and press S, the macro will re-order the table in descending order based on Stock Value. Click on the Quantity column to change some of the values and see if it works.

Now create a button to perform this, as you did with the Highland Borough Council table.

Screen dump 7.13 — showing Lotus 1-2-3 Release 4 window with CH7_9.WK4:

Stock Reference	Quantity	Unit Cost	Minimum Level	Reorder Quantity	Stock Value
C777	12	£0.56	50	30	£6.72
A100	20	£1.89	10	8	£37.80
A224	15	£2.80	12	10	£42.00
A321	15	£2.99	35	20	£44.85
D100	31	£1.62	40	20	£50.22
D220	40	£3.33	30	15	£133.20
B109	15	£9.00	10	5	£135.00
A343	28	*****	20	10	£280.00
B767	23	*****	20	10	£296.24
B200	8	*****	10	10	£440.00
B652	99	£7.01	30	20	£693.99
					£2,160.02

Sort by Values button shown at right.

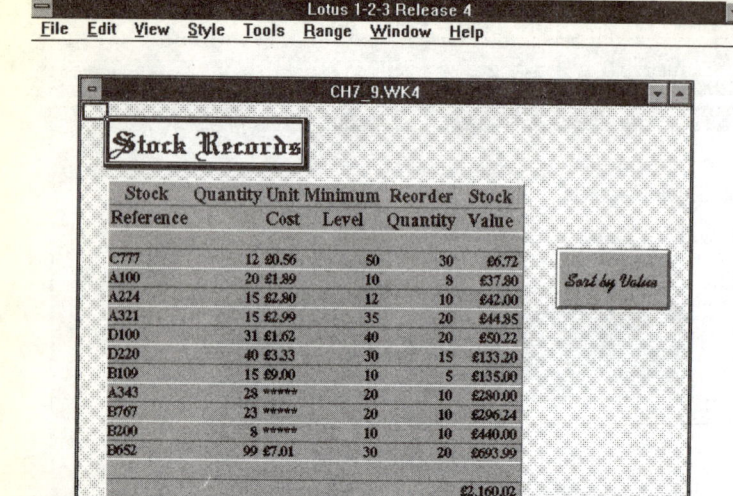

Screen dump 7.13

Screen dump 7.13 shows the final results with a few alterations to the appearance to make it look more interesting.

Save your work before you Exit.

7.9 Chapter summary

This chapter has covered many aspects of database activity although a good deal has been left out. The activities that have been left out are the more advanced features of the database utilities and beyond the scope of a book like this, which has been written as an introduction to the package.

In this chapter, you have:

- defined the term database;
- entered a structured database with records on rows and field titles at the top columns;
- sorted records into logical sequence;

- written a macro by tracing the sequence of commands into a transcript window and then copying them to the spreadsheet;
- created buttons and assigned macros to them;
- set up a Query and extracted data from a defined Input-Range into an Output-Range, using given criteria;
- located a record from an Input-Range, using given criteria;
- deleted records from an Input-Range, using given criteria.

8
MORE ON GRAPHS AND CHARTS

8.1 Aims of this chapter

This chapter aims to give you the opportunity to develop knowledge and skill with regard to graphs and charts beyond those built up in Chapters 4 and 5. Lotus 1-2-3 offers a wide range of facilities in graphs and charts, with varying types and varying presentation. There is also an annotation facility which allows you to indicate information more powerfully.

At this stage in the book it is assumed that the reader knows how to set up a spreadsheet and produce a graph. If you have forgotten any points, refer to previous chapters.

8.2 More on bar charts

This section examines bar charts using a different example from those previously used and allows you to show data in different perspectives. **Screen dump 8.1** shows a spreadsheet of an insurance company's premiums over a given year.

Remember, you cannot simply copy the figures in the spreadsheet. Note the following with regard to the data:

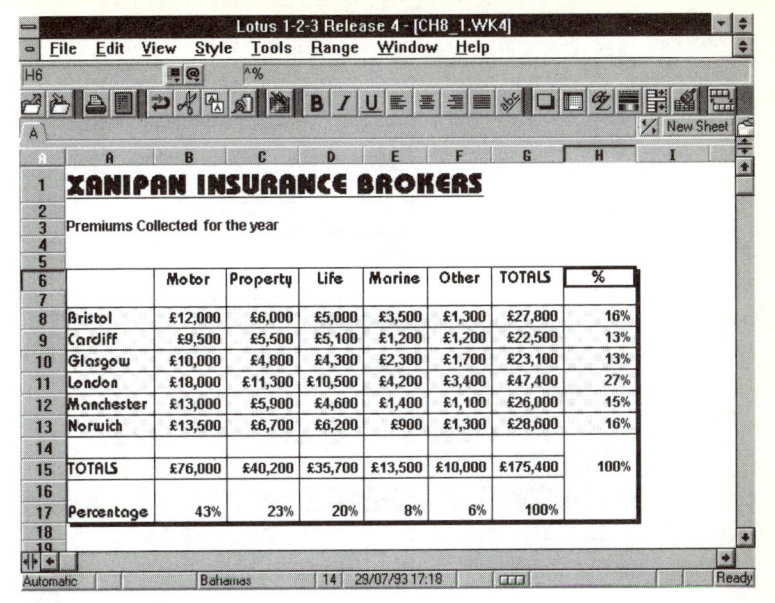

Screen dump 8.1

- Totals are established using the @SUM function.

- Percentages are established using a formula. The formula in cell H8 is: +G8/$G$15 and in cell B17: +B15/$G$15.

The dollar sign in the formula sets an **absolute cell reference**. This was discussed at length in Chapter 6.

- The values that appear in the cells are then formatted to percent, to zero decimal places.

Once you have typed in the spreadsheet, you can work on the graphs.

Screen dump 8.2

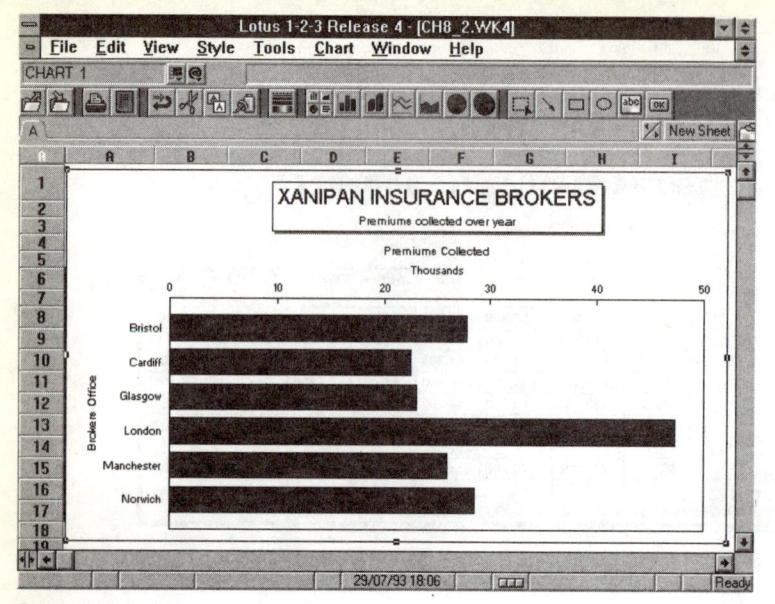

Screen dump 8.2 is no different in construction from the graph set up in Chapter 4, except that it is not three dimensional and it has been rotated. However, it will prove a useful starting-point. As a general principle, use the following procedure for preparing a graph:

First create a set of named ranges as a means of improving the way you create graphs. You will be able to create graph range names without constantly going back to the spreadsheet and highlighting cells.

- Click on Range, then Name.
- Click on the Range box in the Name dialogue box and name the following cell ranges: (Click on the Range box, then click on the button with the left-pointing arrow at the end of the Range box. The dialogue box will temporarily disappear, allowing you to highlight the cells you want to name. When you take your finger off the left-hand mouse button, having highlighted the cells, the range will be automatically written in the Range box, allowing you to click on the Name box and type in the range name. Click on the Add button and repeat.)

Name	Range
LOCATION	A8..A13
TYPES	B6..F6
TOTAL-TYPE	B15..F15
TOTAL-OFFICE	G8..G13
MOTOR	B8..B13
PROPERTY	C8..C13
LIFE	D8..D13
MARINE	E8..E13
OTHER	F8..F13
BRISTOL	B8..F8
CARDIFF	B9..F9
GLASGOW	B10..F10
LONDON	B11..F11
MANCHESTER	B12..F12
NORWICH	B13..F13

[If you are a Release 1 user, position the cell pointer in cell A20 and from the Range pull-down menu select Name, and then Paste Table. Type in the table defining the ranges and their name in A20, and you will get a list of these ranges. Check that they are correct.]

This method of naming ranges is designed to conform to good spreadsheet practice by making the setting up of the graphs easier to follow.

[If you are a Release 1 user: Click the cell pointer on any blank cell. Pull down the Graph menu, select New and accept the graph name as GRAPH1.]

● Click on the Graph SmartIcon. (Or click on Tools, then Chart.) Draw a frame to occupy a large part of the screen.

A line graph will appear with the Graph pull-down menus and new SmartIcons. The first job will be to define the X-range and A-range for the axes.

● Click on the Bar Chart SmartIcon.

● Click on Chart, then Ranges. Click on X-Axis labels in the Series box of the Ranges dialogue box. In the Range box, type: LOCATION. The click on A-Data A in the Series box, click again on the Range box, and type: TOTAL-OFFICE. Then click on the OK button.

At this stage you have a single Y-variable which is defined as the A-series with the data contained in the named range TOTAL-OFFICE. Give the graph a title. (Click on the Title box in the graph and then double click.)

    Line 1:   XANIPAN INSURANCE BROKERS
    Line 2:   Premiums collected over year

- Click the OK button. Then click on the Type SmartIcon. (Or click on Chart, then Type.) Click the Horizontal Orientation box, then click on the OK button.

You now have the basics of the graph. Next you must label the axis.

- Click on Chart, then Axis, then X-Axis.
- Click on the Axis title box and type the title: Brokers Office. Then click on the OK button.
- Repeat for the Y-Axis typing in the label: Premiums Collected. Then click on the OK button.
- Click on the Data A box and press the **Delete** key on your keyboard. It will be deleted.

8.3 Multiple bar charts

The problem with the graph as it stands is that it fails to show all the information available in the spreadsheet. The totals show which brokers are the largest but the graph does not break down the size of the business in each category as shown in the spreadsheet.

Look at **Screen dump 8.3**. Instead of showing the totals for each office, this shows the size of each category for each office.

There are in fact new differences between the two graphs beyond the stark appearances. The titles are still the same and the X-Axis has not been altered. One problem that has been taken away from you is the size of the scale. If you observe the Y-Axis you will see that the scale ranges from zero at the bottom to 18,000 at the top. In **Screen dump 8.2** the scale range was from zero to 50,000. Lotus 1-2-3 works all this out for you.

Each City broker is represented by five bars, one for each category of insurance. The bar for each insurance category is explained at

MORE ON GRAPHS AND CHARTS

the bottom of the screen by the LEGENDS. This is an extra you ought to put on your graph if an observer is to understand what is being shown.

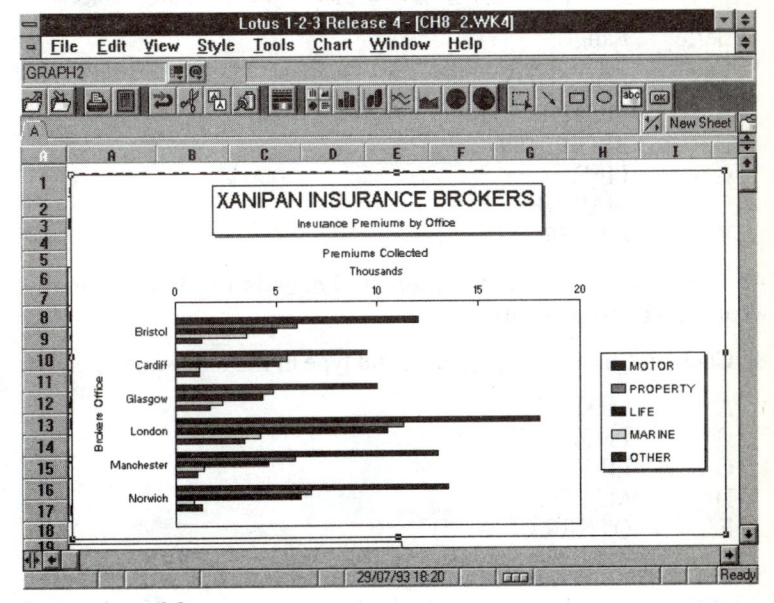

Screen dump 8.3

[If you are a Release 1 user: Pull down the Graph menu, select New, and allow it the name GRAPH2.]

- Click on Chart, then Name, accept the name CHART 1. Click on cancel.

- Reduce the size of your graph by dragging the sides and move it to a position below the table. Click on a cell in the table.

- Click on the Chart SmartIcon, draw a new frame to occupy the whole screen.

- Click on the Bar Chart SmartIcon, then on the Type SmartIcon.

- Click on Horizontal Orientation, then on the OK button. Click on Chart, then Headings, and in the Title box type:

    Line 1: XANIPAN INSURANCE BROKERS
    Line 2: Insurance Premiums by Office

Click on Chart, then Axis, then: X-Axis, and type in: Brokers Office. Repeat for the Y-Axis: Premiums Collected.

Click on Chart, then Ranges, and type in the following ranges:

Series	Range
X	LOCATION
A	MOTOR
B	PROPERTY
C	LIFE
D	MARINE
E	OTHER

All that now remains is to enter the Legends needed to identify what each bar represents.

- Click on Chart, then Legends, and type in the following legends:

A	MOTOR
B	PROPERTY
C	LIFE
D	MARINE
E	OTHER

Now view the graph to see what you have achieved. Use the 3-D bar chart SmartIcon for a different look at your graph. If you are a Release 4 user then resize the chart and move it to a clear space on the spreadsheet. [If you are a pre-Release 4 user, click on Chart, then Name and enter the name GRAPH2, then select Rename. This stores the graph as a separate file that can be used by other packages such as CorelDraw and WordPerfect.]

Because you used named ranges rather than cell locations to identify ranges, the entering of both series and legend titles became simple and quite logical.

Compare your graph with **Screen dump 8.3.**

MORE ON GRAPHS AND CHARTS

8.4 Changing the perspectives of your graph

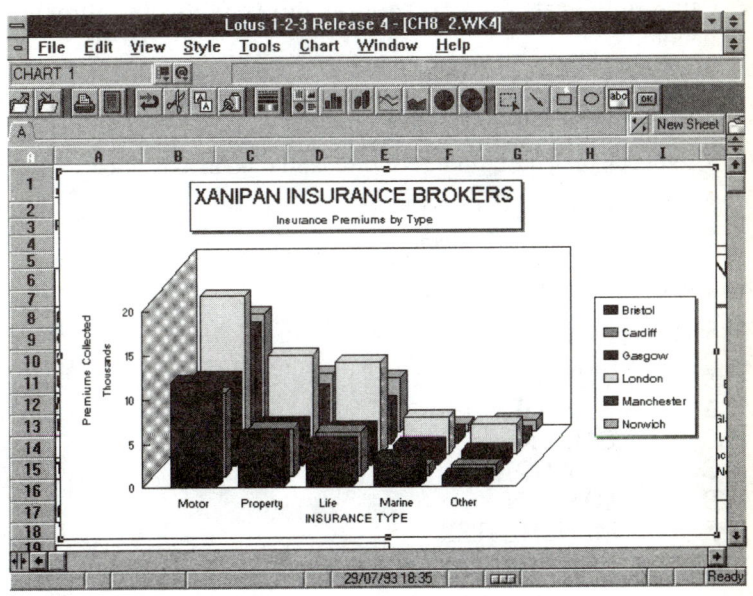

Screen dump 8.4

You now have a graph that shows, for each office, the premiums collected for each category of insurance. Suppose that you want to show for each category of insurance how much each office has collected. **Screen dump 8.4** shows an example of this.

In this instance the X-Axis variable is the category of insurance while the Y-Axis variables are the six city offices. You can now see the relative importance of each category of insurance more clearly and how much each office has contributed to the total.

To achieve this perspective of the data you need to alter X and Y variables as well as the legends. You will also have to change the title on the X-Axis. The rest will be much the same as before.

- Create a third graph area.
- Click on the 3-D Bar Chart SmartIcon. Select the chart where two bars are in front of two larger bars.
- Click on Chart, then Headings, and type in the following headings:

  Line 1: XANIPAN INSURANCE BROKERS
  Line 2: Insurance Premiums by Type

- Then click on Chart, then Axis, etc. and type in axis titles:

  X   INSURANCE TYPE
  Y   Premiums Collected.

- Click on Chart, then Ranges as follows:

Series	Range
X	TYPES
A	BRISTOL
B	CARDIFF
C	GLASGOW
D	LONDON
E	MANCHESTER
F	NORWICH.

- Now click on Chart, then Legend and type in the Legends, as above.

Your graph should now show the desired result. The 3-D effect works better here because the X-Axis titles are smaller. However, you may find some of the bars a little obscured. In the next section you will see a possible alternative to this.

Resize and move your chart to a blank area of the spreadsheet.

8.5 Stacked bar chart

Looking at **Screen dump 8.4** you may not be satisfied that the reader can tell at a glance the size of each category of insurance. Observe the stacked bar chart in **Screen dump 8.5** to see the data in a different way.

MORE ON GRAPHS AND CHARTS

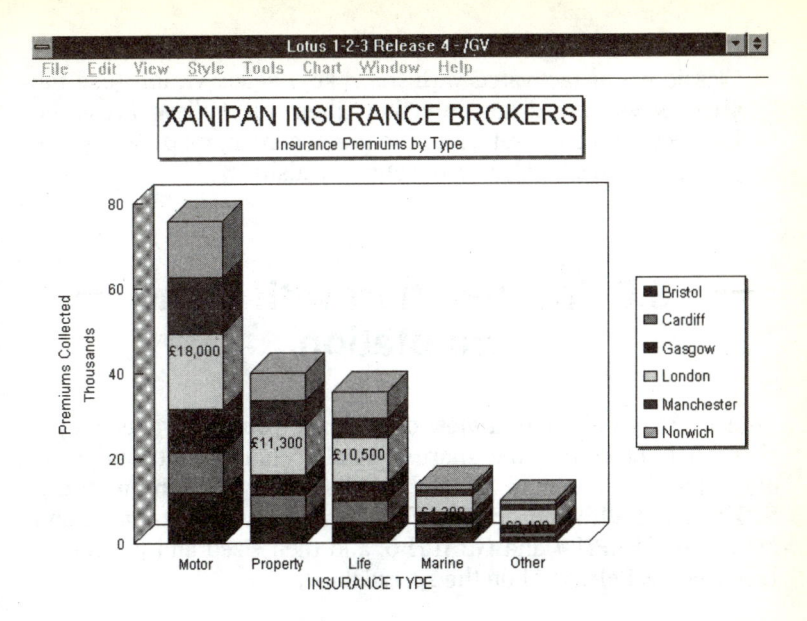

Screen dump 8.5

This graph uses one bar for each category on the X-Axis while splitting up the bar into components for each of the Y variables.

- Click on the Types SmartIcon, then the Stacked Bar Icon, then click on the OK button.

Everything has been done for you in terms of the scaling.

You can label particular parts of your graph. In this example, you will bring attention to the premiums collected by the London office.

- Click on Chart, then Data Labels.

- Highlight D in the Series box, click on the Range of labels box, type in London, and click on the OK button.

You can now see the effect for yourself. You could, of course, do this for all labels, but your chart might look too congested.

- If you are a Release 1 user press function key F11 to view your graph.

- If you are a Release 4 user, click on the graph and from the Classic menu (activated with the / key) select Graph (use the arrow keys), press the Enter key, then select View. Press the **Esc** key 3 times to return to the graph screen, resize and move your graph to a blank area of your spreadsheet.

8.6 The pie chart with some annotation

In order to get a different view of the data, you can produce a pie chart that shows first the share of total premium contribution by office and then the share of total premium by type. **Screen dump 8.6** shows both such graphs. These graphs were generated and named as GRAPH 4 and GRAPH 5, and then sized and positioned [inserted for Release 1] on the spreadsheet.

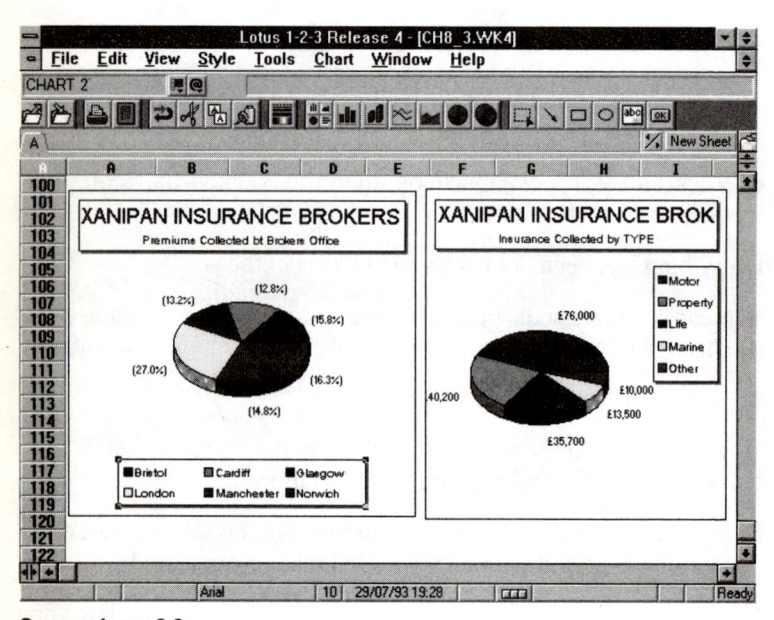

Screen dump 8.6

You can see at a glance the relative contribution each has made to the total. In the pie that shows Insurance by Type, the motor segment has been removed from the rest of the pie like a slice of cake being cut; a technique called "exploding". This can be extremely useful if you want to highlight one particular segment.

You will also notice in **Screen dump 8.7** that text has been added to indicate that London is a record high. This was created by the Annotate facility.

In order to create a pie chart, a little less information is required than was needed for the bar charts. All you need is an X variable to determine what each portion of the pie represents and a variable to determine which figures to measure against, plus some titles at the top.

- Create a new chart. Click on the 3-D Pie Chart SmartIcon.

- Set Ranges as:

    Series   Range

    X-Legend   LOCATION
    A-Slice   TOTAL-OFFICE.

- Set the following Titles as:

    Line 1: XANIPAN INSURANCE BROKERS
    Line 2: Premiums Collected by Brokers Office.

If the figures are unclear, click on one of them. It will become surrounded by four black squares. Click on the right mouse button, then on Font & Attributes. Click on 12 in the Size box in the Font & Attributes dialogue box, then click on the OK button.

When adding annotated objects to a chart, you need to be aware that these too are floating objects. This means that if you alter the size of the chart or move it, the annotated objects remain where they are. It is wise, therefore, to place such objects on to charts when you are certain about the size and final location of your chart.

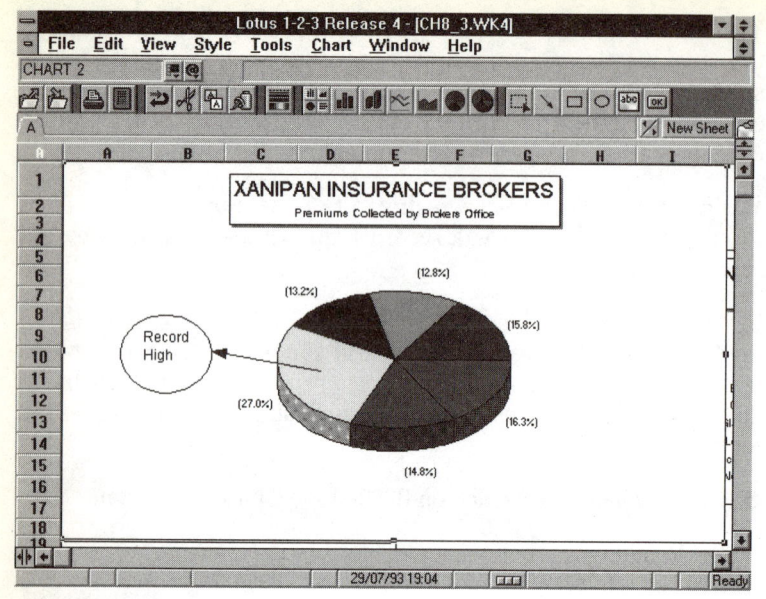

Screen dump 8.7

- Click on the Arrow SmartIcon. The printer becomes a black cross.

- Now position the black cross in the pie segment for London (27%) and, keeping the mouse button depressed, drag a line from this segment. When you have a line of the required length, double click your mouse to see the arrow head appear.

This arrow now becomes an OBJECT. It can be moved if you feel you have made a mess. A single click over an object will cause small boxes to appear along it, indicating that the object is the subject of editing. If the object is the subject and you press your delete key, it will disappear. In fact, while an object is the subject, you can carry out editing activities via the Edit pull-down menu. By double-clicking on the arrow you can produce a Lines & Color dialogue box and change its appearance.

- Now create a circle at the end of the arrow by clicking on the Circle SmartIcon and then using the mouse to control the size of the object, as you did with the arrow.

Text can be added in much the same way.

MORE ON GRAPHS AND CHARTS

- Click on the 'abc' SmartIcon, click on the graph, and type in the word: Record.
- Now move the object with your mouse to the desired location and double click.
- Reduce its size and move the object to its required location in the same way as you would any other object.
- Repeat this for the word: High.

This can all take some dexterity and practice, but adding annotated objects to your graph allows a good deal of imaginative additions to be made. With Release 4 you will have a problem when you resize and move your graph. The annotated objects will remain where they were originally created and stay the same size. Consequently, such objects will have to be moved along with the chart or created on the graphs when you have decided on the permanent location of the chart.

- If you are a Release 4 user resize and move your graph. In doing so, either delete the annotated objects or move them as well. With such annotated objects, there is no reason why they cannot overlap on to the spreadsheet area of your screen.

This has completed the first pie chart. Now go on to create the next pie chart.

Set ranges as:

Range	Range
X	TYPES
A	TOTAL-TYPE.

- Set the titles as:

  Line 1: XANIPAN INSURANCE BROKERS
  Line 2: Insurance Collected by TYPE.

Finally, try to produce what appears in **Screen dump 8.6** by positioning the graph side by side.

At this stage save your work. The entire spreadsheet, when saved, will also hold all your graphs.

Before going on to the next section, you are advised to practise calling up different graphs, altering some of the numerical data on the spreadsheet to some of your own figures and viewing the differences that occur. Remember, you can position graphs next to the spreadsheet, allowing you to see any changes made to the graphs as you alter them. When you have finished experimenting with this, you will need to retrieve your present file in order to complete the chapter material.

8.7 Line graphs

In this next section you will go on to develop a different set of graphs for which the data you already have is not really appropriate. By means of extension, you will set up an additional table of data showing the number of insurance claims made over the year, as well as the amount paid out to those claiming. Examine **Screen dump 8.8** to see what you need to set up the initial data.

MONTH	CLAIMS	PAYOUTS
January	147	£14,700
February	152	£15,000
March	133	£13,200
April	133	£12,900
May	112	£11,350
June	123	£12,190
July	124	£12,200
August	124	£12,350
September	135	£13,350
October	144	£14,500
November	145	£12,550
December	146	£14,600

Screen dump 8.8

The table has been placed to the right of the other table and shows two variables: number of claims and amount paid out, against one time variable.

MORE ON GRAPHS AND CHARTS

- Press function key **F5**, type J1 in the second box, then press the OK button.

- Type in the data exactly as it appears in **Screen dump 8.8**. There are no formulae in this table. As a quick tip, try this: type January in cell J7, then click on the tick. Position the pointer on cell J7, press the left mouse button and highlight cells J7 to J18. Click on Range, then Fill by Example. The months will automatically be filled in.

Make any alterations to the style you feel appropriate. An exact likeness to **Screen dump 8.8** is not necessary for this exercise.

As has now become normal practice, name three of the ranges that will be needed to set up the graphs:

Range location	Range name
J7..J18	MONTH
K8..K18	CLAIMS
L8..L18	PAYOUTS.

- Draw a new graph, as you have done before.

- Click on the Type SmartIcon and click on 3D Line.

- Of the two variants available, select the one where one line appears to overlap the other.

The plain Line option can be tried later.

You now need to determine the variables. As is normal, you want to see how things have changed over time, so use MONTH as the X-Axis Series. In the first graph of this section, you will be looking at how the number of claims has changed over the year. As the A-Data Series, use CLAIMS. (Click on Chart, then Ranges.)

Give the axes the following titles:

X Title	MONTH
Y Title	NUMBER OF CLAIMS.

As with the bar charts, the scale has been worked out for you. You can see quite clearly how the number of claims made alters over the year.

You are now in a position to enter the amount in £s claimed over the year and place these details on to the same graph. Doing this will simply mean adding another variable. It will alter the scales quite considerably and you will need to label the Y-Axis to inform observers that it is used to measure both number of claims and amount in £s.

- Click on Chart, then Ranges, highlight B-Data in the Series box, then type PAYOUTS in the Range box.

- Now take a look at the graph.

The problem should be an obvious one: you are unable to get a proper view of the number of claims because the Y-Axis covers too wide a range; from just 114 to over 15,000. You will need to reduce this range if you are to get a readable graph.

As a solution, you could express the amount claimed in hundreds. This would reduce the range of numbers from 112 to 150. This will mean, however, creating a new range of values from which to plot on the spreadsheet. The method will involve creating a new column of figures and then hiding it from view.

- Go back to your spreadsheet and enter into cell M7 the formula +L7/100, and copy this formula to the range M8..M18.

- Click on Range, then Name and click on PAYOUTS in the Existing named ranges box and change the range to M7..M18.

- Now hide the newly created range. You can do this by clicking on Style, then Hide. Simply enter the range name PAYOUTS, and click on the OK button. The entire column is now hidden. You can open it again with the pointer in the column letter tabs.

You should now be able to see why it is useful to show amounts claimed in thousands of £s against the number of claims. This graph now needs some alterations to improve its appearance.

- Click on Chart, then Axis, then Y-Axis. Amend the Axis title to read: Number of Claims/£000s.

- Now click on Chart, then Legend. Type in new Legend entries:

    A   Number of Claims
    B   Amount Claimed.

MORE ON GRAPHS AND CHARTS

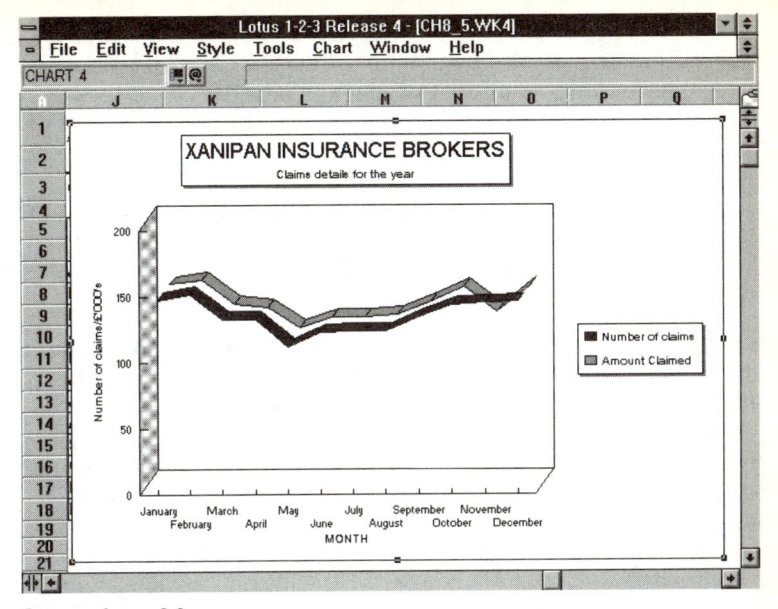

Screen dump 8.9

The graph, as shown in **Screen dump 8.9** (yours may not be quite the same; see below), has a three dimensional effect with two ribbon-like lines representing the two variables. The one in front (the A range) is the number of claims and the one behind (the B range) the amount claimed.

Before going into the next section, it is worth examining a method by which you can determine the scale on the axis rather than having it automatically set. By example, you will set the Y-Axis to go from zero up to 100, an extension at both the upper and lower ends of the axis.

- Click on Chart, then Axis, then Y-Axis.
- [For Release 1 users set the Scale axis option to Manual.]
- In the Scale manually box, click on the Lower limit box and type in a new value 0 (zero); similarly change the Upper limit to 200. Then click on the OK button.
- Now see the effect.

Before moving on, look at the other line graphs that are available. Two others are worth examination. Resize your chart area and move the chart to a blank area of your spreadsheet.

8.8 Scatter graphs or xy graphs

Such graphs are used to plot one variable against another in an attempt to see if there is any correlation or relationship between them. For example, in the line graph you have just produced, you plotted both number of claims and amount claimed against Time. You could just as easily have plotted the number of claims against the amounts claimed to see if there is any relationship between these two variables. In this case, you will see that they tend to increase together.

Screen dump 8.3 shows such a graph that has been added to the sheet, where the relationship can be seen. Simply plot one variable (X) against another variable (Y). Time does not matter in this case. In practice, such graphs would be used with a much larger amount of data where the relationship might not be so obvious.

It can be seen that when the number of claims is high, so is the amount claimed, demonstrating positive correlation. Another relationship could be the opposite. For example, if you were to plot rainfall against temperature, you might find that on days when rainfall is high, there is a tendency for temperatures to be lower. This is called negative correlation.

Where there is a correlation between two variables, it is possible to use such relationships to predict events. For example, if there is shown to be correlation of a positive kind between temperature and rainfall, you could work out the likely average temperature given a certain amount of rainfall. Lotus 1-2-3 has an Advanced Maths utility that can assist here; a topic beyond the scope of a book of this nature.

MORE ON GRAPHS AND CHARTS

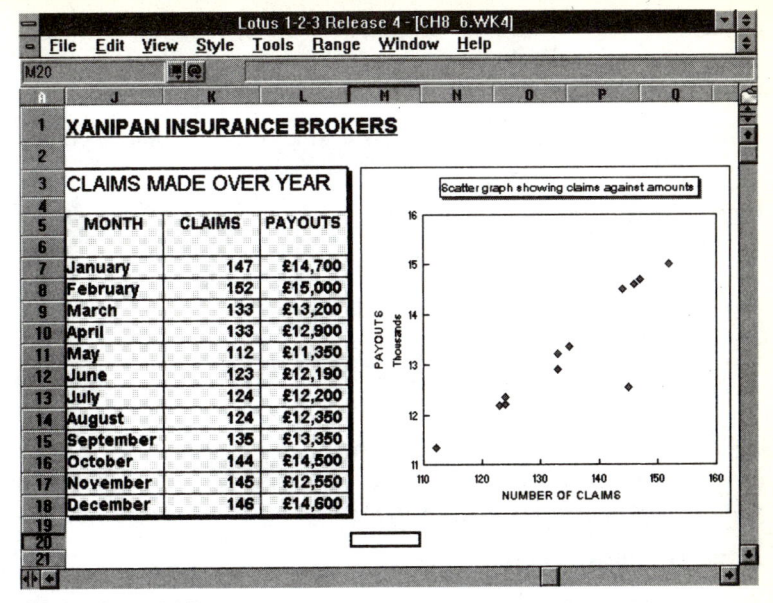

Screen dump 8.10

MONTH	CLAIMS	PAYOUTS
January	147	£14,700
February	152	£15,000
March	133	£13,200
April	133	£12,900
May	112	£11,350
June	123	£12,190
July	124	£12,200
August	124	£12,350
September	135	£13,350
October	144	£14,500
November	145	£12,550
December	146	£14,600

- Highlight cells K7 to L18.
- Draw a new graph, as you have done before.

Lotus 1-2-3 makes an instant attempt to draw a graph for you and should default to a line graph. (This depends on the last graph type you have drawn.)

- Click on the Type SmartIcon and select the XY option.

Look at **Screen dump 8.10** and the titles that have been given. Click again on the Type SmartIcon.

You will see a set of six possible graphs of this kind. The one in **Screen dump 8.10** is bottom right, where the plotted points are not joined. This technically, is the right choice for a scatter graph.

- Click on the appropriate XY graph and look at the result.

Next you must resize and move the graph to an appropriate part of the spreadsheet. [For Release 1 you will add the graph to the sheet. Make sure the hidden numbers used to create the line graph are not written over.]

Before moving to the next chapter, try experimenting with this graph to see the effect that changing the data might have. Try the following:

- Create numbers in the table so that as the number of claims increases the amounts claimed decrease.
- Randomise the figures so that there is no apparent correlation between them.

8.9 Chapter summary

This chapter has set out to cover many of the graphics creation aspects of Lotus 1-2-3. It has not covered all aspects and will leave you to investigate other aspects more fully.

In this chapter you have:

- determined X and Y axes;
- set up a simple bar chart;
- constructed a multiple bar chart;
- typed in titles and legends on a graph;
- altered the perspective of graphs;
- constructed a stack bar chart;
- constructed pie charts;
- added annotated objects to a graph;
- constructed line graphs with single and multiple variables;
- constructed three-dimensional graphs;
- altered the scaling of an axis;
- constructed scatter graphs.

9
THREE-DIMENSIONAL SPREADSHEETS

9.1 Aims of this chapter

This chapter will introduce you to the idea of working with multiple spreadsheets. Lotus 1-2-3 refers to the concept as 3-D, or three-dimensional.

The principle is that a spreadsheet has columns and rows and so is two-dimensional. A third dimension is added when you have a stack of sheets one on top of another. Lotus 1-2-3 will allow you to have 256 such sheets, although filling all these up will be restricted by the amount of available memory. The idea works rather like a book, in that a single page of the book reads across and down, while a whole series of sheets makes up a book.

With respect to the spreadsheet, each layer will be called a sheet and the whole collection of these sheets will be called the spreadsheet.

In earlier chapters you have come across the idea of having more than one spreadsheet open at any one time. You can cascade the display of spreadsheets to create a layered effect similar to what you will see in this chapter. The difference, however, is that each sheet in a multi-layered spreadsheet is permanently connected and they will all load when the spreadsheet is open. It will also be considerably easier to link formulae in one sheet with data stored on another.

9.2 Looking at multiple sheets

- In a blank screen, click on View, [Window for Release 1], then Split, and in the Split dialogue box, click on Perspective, then on the OK button.

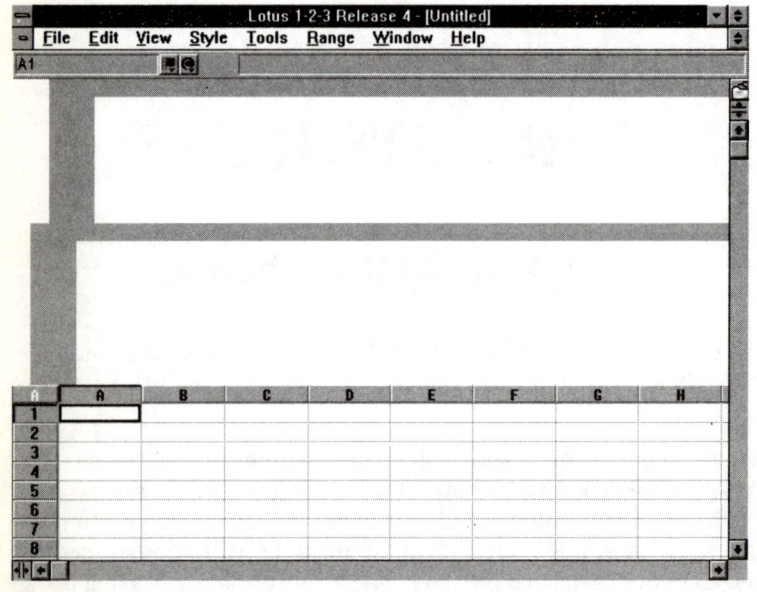

Screen dump 9.1

At this stage you see three sheets on your screen as in **Screen dump 9.1**. [The screen dump has had the SmartIcons and Status bar switched off by clicking on View, then Set View Preferences, and clicking on the appropriate Show in 1-2-3 boxes.]

The sheet in front is labelled Sheet 'A' and is the only active Sheet in the spreadsheet. This chapter will require you to work with four sheets to show you how Lotus 1-2-3 works in a three-dimensional environment.

- Click on Edit, then Insert. [Worksheet in Release 1.] In the Insert dialogue box, click on Sheet, then After (to indicate that you want the sheets to appear after A: namely B, C, D and E), and set Quantity to 4.

- Then click on the OK button.

Screen dump 9.2 shows sheets B, C, D displayed at the same time. As you will observe, they are all labelled with row numbers and column letters. The perspective view of the spreadsheet will show exactly three sheets at a time; Sheet A has not been lost.

Although you have selected four sheets you will see later in this chapter that you can always add or delete sheets to and from these and place them or delete them before, after and between other sheets, rather like adding or removing pages in a loose-leaf book.

The highlighted cell should now be A1 of sheet B. The cell indicator in the control panel refers to this cell location B:A1. As a useful tip, think of a cell A:A1 as being directly in front, and cell C:A1 as directly behind.

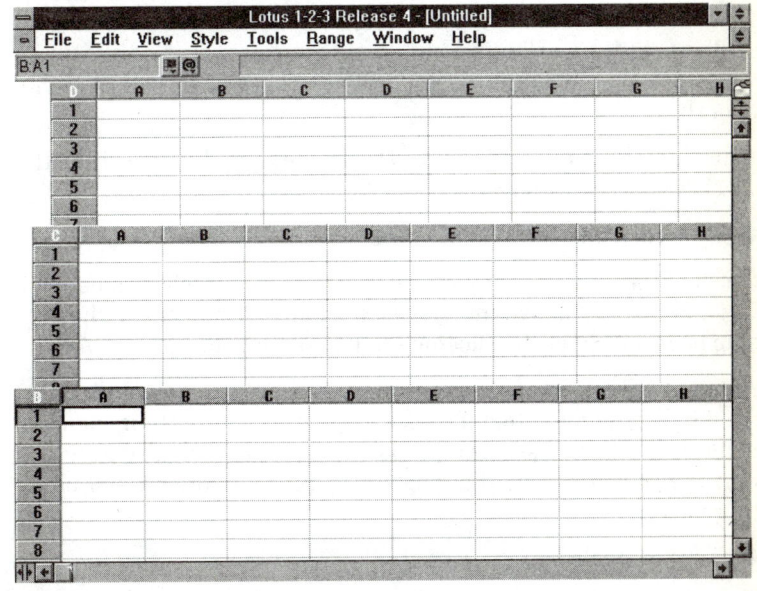

Screen dump 9.2

- Hold down **Ctrl** and press **Page Up** to move to sheet C.
- Now hold down the **Ctrl** key and press the **Page Down** key to move back to sheet B, then to sheet A. (You will observe that sheet D no longer appears on your screen.)

Within each sheet the right, left, up, and down arrow keys are used to navigate within a sheet. Experiment further by moving between sheets and within sheets until you are familiar with the idea.

You should now see what is meant by the concept of a three-dimensional spreadsheet. We now have columns with letter headings A, B, C, D...; rows with numbers 1, 2, 3, 4, 5...; and layers of sheets A:, B:, C:, D: ... . The next stage is to see what can be done with this extra dimension.

9.3 Setting up the first sheet

This example will begin by setting up sheet A with a Sales Analysis table for Europa Components to different countries in the month of October. When building up any single sheet, working with the perspective mode on will prove awkward because you can only view six lines in a sheet at a time, so you will need to clear this when typing up a sheet.

- Using the **Ctrl** and **Page Down** keys make sure that the current working sheet is Sheet A.

- Now click on View, then Clear Split.

On the Release 4 screen you will see a set of worksheet tabs A, B, C, D, and E just above the spreadsheet area. You can use these to skip between sheets by clicking on the relevant sheet.

Although you will only see one sheet in the conventional way, you need to bear in mind that the other sheets (B, C and D) are still resident. It is rather like having a book open at a particular page and only being able to see that page in spite of the others still being there.

- Type in labels:

cell	label
A1	EUROPA COMPONENTS
A3	Sales Analysis by Country
C3	OCTOBER
A5	Country
B5 and B6	Sales Value
C5	Percentage

- Widen the columns, where necessary. And make the title and labels more prominent.
- Type in the 9 countries in the range of cells from A8 to A16, as they appear in **Screen dump 9.3**.

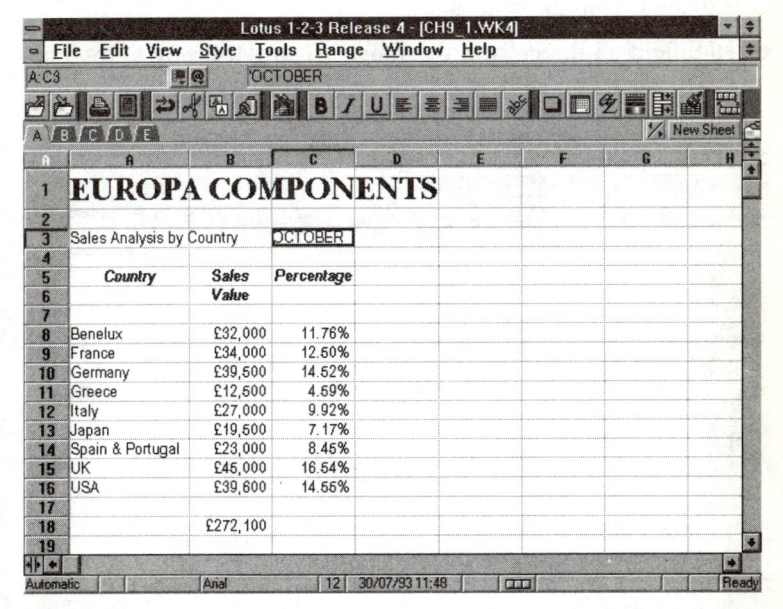

Screen dump 9.3

- Highlight column B and Number Format the column as Currency, to zero decimal places. Highlight column C and Number Format the columns as Percent, to 2 decimal places.
- Type in the sales values in the range B8 to B16, as in **Screen dump 9.3**.
- Highlight the range of sales values in cells B8 to B16 and, by clicking on Range, then Name, name the range: SALES.
- Now click on cell B18 and type in: @SUM(SALES).
- Click on cell C8 and type in the formula: +B8/B$18. Note how the row 18 in the formula has been fixed as absolute. This will allow you to copy the formula to cells C9 to C16.

Observe **Screen dump 9.3** to make sure that you have a similar set-up.

9.4 Copying between sheets

Your next objective will be to copy the entire contents of Sheet A to Sheet B. The principle is no different from copying from a range of cells to another in the same sheet.

- Highlight all the cells in the range A1 to C18, copy to the clipboard, click on Tab B, and Paste to Sheet B.

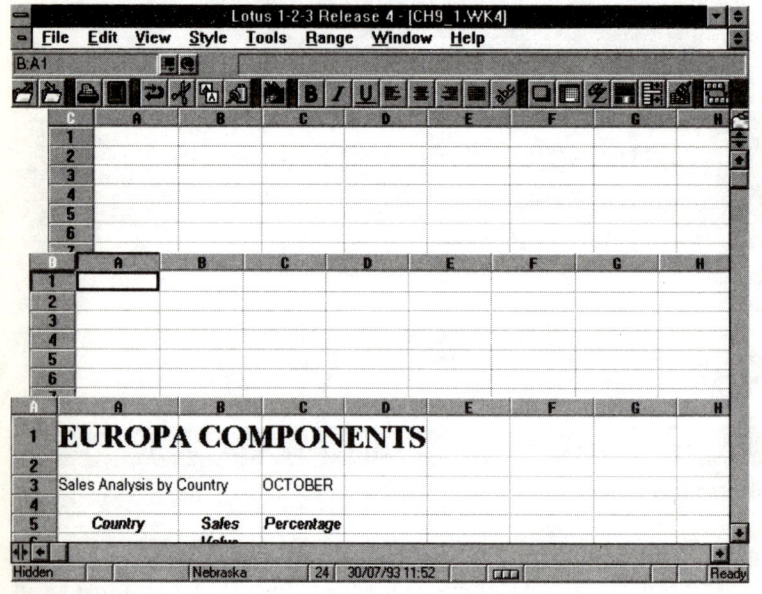

Screen dump 9.4

Screen dump 9.4 shows sheets split in perspective.

You will have noticed that Sheets A and B have different column widths so that the data does not fit correctly in Sheet B.

- Click on Style, then Worksheet Defaults. In the dialogue box is a box headed Other. Make sure the Group mode box has an X. This solves the problem immediately.

In most cases, this is set as the default and you would not need to make any alterations.

9.5 Entering three-dimensional formulae

- Make sure you are in Sheet B and remove the perspective, by clicking on View, then on Clear Split. [Window pull-down menu for Release 1.]

Examine **Screen dump 9.5** and make the necessary alteration to the label in C3 by altering the month to NOVEMBER, and then type in new sales values in the range B8 to B16.

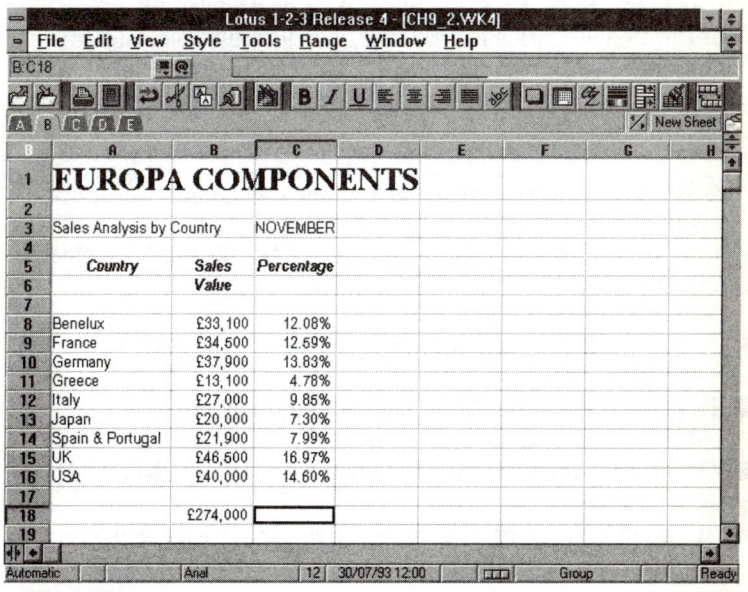

	A	B	C	D
1	**EUROPA COMPONENTS**			
2				
3	Sales Analysis by Country		NOVEMBER	
4				
5	Country	Sales	Percentage	
6		Value		
7				
8	Benelux	£33,100	12.08%	
9	France	£34,500	12.59%	
10	Germany	£37,900	13.83%	
11	Greece	£13,100	4.78%	
12	Italy	£27,000	9.85%	
13	Japan	£20,000	7.30%	
14	Spain & Portugal	£21,900	7.99%	
15	UK	£46,500	16.97%	
16	USA	£40,000	14.60%	
17				
18		£274,000		

Screen dump 9.5

You will now type into Sheet B a formula that works out the difference between sales in the current month of November with those of the previous month of October, in other words the differences of the values in the respective B6 cells.

- First widen column D. (Because the Group mode is set enabled, it will automatically set the column widths of **all** sheets.)

- Type in the new column heading so that "Sales Change" appears in D5 and "on Month" appears in D6. Also centre and embolden this new heading to imitate the existing headings. Highlight column D and Number Format the column as currency, to zero decimal places.

Now you are ready to use a formula that links with the other sheet.

- In cell D8 type in the formula +B8–A:B8.

Cell B8 contains the monthly sales for Benelux in the current sheet for November. Cell A:B8 is in Sheet A, as its prefix implies, and contains the Benelux sales for October. The formula calculates the difference in sales between the two months. A negative figure would imply a fall in sales between the two months; a positive figure implies an increase.

Now you need to do the same for the remaining countries. Because the relative positions of the remaining countries all remain the same, you will be able to copy and paste the formula already entered to the remaining countries.

- Click on cell D8, click on Edit, then Copy.

- Highlight cells D9 to D16, click on Edit, then Paste.

- Now type in the totalling function in cell D18: @SUM (D8..D16).

Examine **Screen dump 9.6** to see Sheet B with a more interesting appearance.

Because the multiple sheets have been set up as group mode, any alterations to the Style and Presentation of any one sheet causes the same effect on the rest. This change also applies to column widths and row heights. Any insertions or alterations to labels, numbers, formulae and functions will only alter the single sheet and not the rest.

THREE-DIMENSIONAL SPREADSHEETS

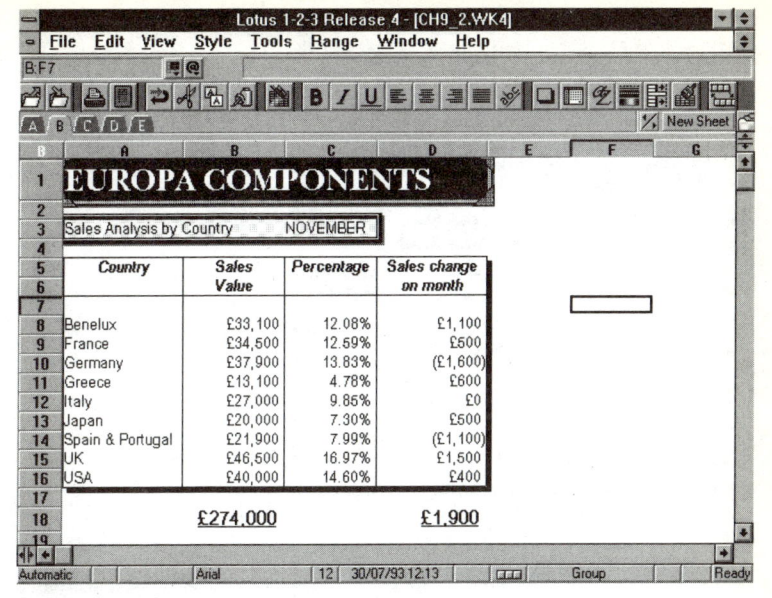

Screen dump 9.6

- Change the style of Sheet B. (Click on Style, then Gallery, and choose a style.)
- Now hop between Sheets A and B to see the effect.

Observe how the style settings have changed in all sheets.

9.6 Building up a history

The next stage is to copy the contents of Sheet B to Sheet C to give sales for December.

- Highlight the entire range (cells A1 to D18) of Sheet B. Click on Edit, then Copy.
- Click on cell A1 in Sheet C, click on Edit, then Paste.

Screen dump 9.7 shows the likely result with styles as before.

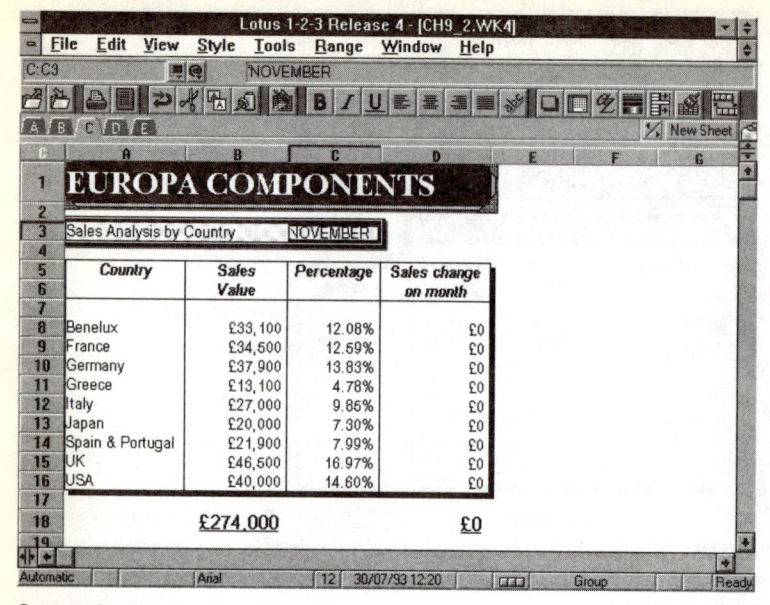

Screen dump 9.7

You will notice that the "Sales Change on Month" column shows all zeros. This is exactly to be expected because monthly figures in both Sheet B and Sheet C are at present the same. This confirms that the formulae have been copied successfully as well as the numbers and labels.

- Make sure you are working in Sheet C.

- Change the label in C3 to DECEMBER.

- Type in the data shown in **Screen dump 9.8**, altering the monthly sales figures, and observe what happens to the figures in the "Sales Change on Month" column as you work through it.

The percentage figures will also change as the new sales values are entered. However, these are based on two dimensional formulae.

THREE-DIMENSIONAL SPREADSHEETS

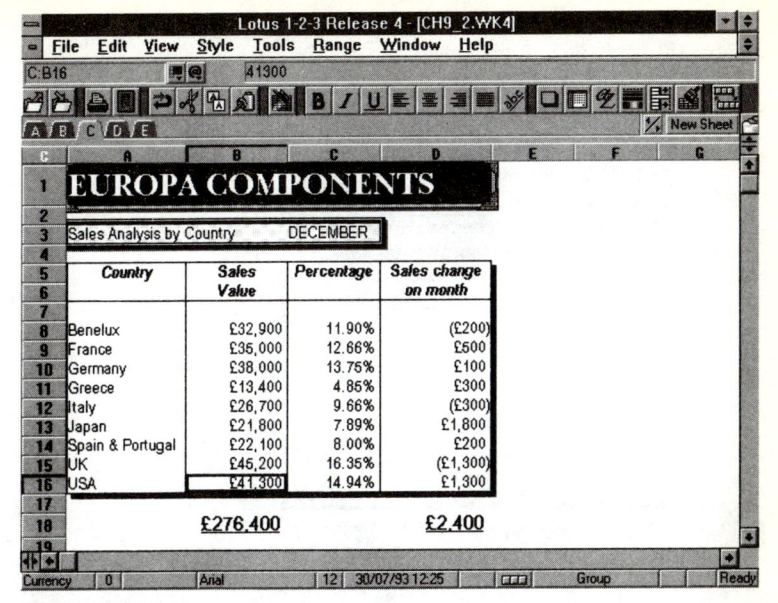

Screen dump 9.8

You should now be able to appreciate that the task becomes easier as you work through the months. You may, for example, want to go on with this for many more months.

9.7 Summarising the sheets

The next task is to produce a summary sheet that adds all the monthly sales figures together. You could enter this, for example, as Sheet Z, giving yourself room for many more months after December. However, this is unnecessary, as you will always have the opportunity to insert sheets between existing ones in the same way as you would insert a new column or row within a single sheet.

Screen dump 9.9 shows the desired effect where the Sales Value figures are the totals for each of the three months you have already entered on Sheets A, B, and C.

LOTUS 1–2–3 WINDOWS

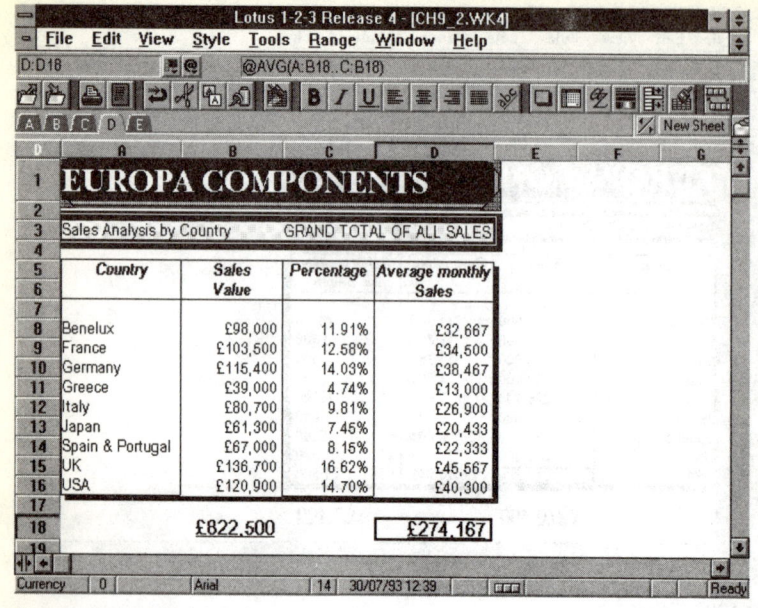

Screen dump 9.9

The figures in column B will sum up all monthly sales from October to December, and Column D will calculate the average sales for each country over the three months. In both cases, the formulae will be calculated on figures across more than one sheet.

- Copy the entire contents of Sheet C to Sheet D, without using the perspective screen set-up.

- Alter the label in cell C3 to: GRAND TOTAL OF ALL SALES.

- Alter the label in cell D5 to read: Average Monthly and in cell D6 to read: Sales.

- Highlight cells B8 to B16 and press the **Delete** key.

- Highlight cells D8 to D16 and press the **Delete** key.

- Click on cell B8 and type in the formula: @SUM (A:B8..C:B8).

- Copy the function in cell B8 to the range B9..B16.

The function in cell B8 has added together the contents of the three values in B8 for Sheets A, B, and C, in a three-dimensional sense. It would now be easy to add another sheet for another month between Sheet C and D and then include this extra month in the formula. Simply staying in Sheet D and inserting a new sheet would have the desired effect. (Click on Edit, then Insert, then Sheet, then Before, then click on the OK button.)

As a further demonstration of how the three-dimensional effect works, you will calculate a formula that works out the average monthly sales value of the three months' sales value figures.

- Click on cell D8 and type in the function @AVG (A:B8..C:B8), then copy this formula from cell D8 to the range of cells D9 to D16.

You now have two sets of formulae that make use of the three-dimensional effect. If you are unsure as to what has happened, then browse through the range of cells where the formulae have been set to see how it has worked.

- In order to gain a better appreciation of this, insert a sheet between C and D for the month of January.

- Now copy the contents of Sheet C (December) to the new Sheet D (January) and make the relevant amendments to the text in cell C3 and Sale Values.

- Make the necessary alterations to the formulae in the summary sheet which should, after the insertion, be Sheet E.

In Release 4 you can name each Sheet, rather than relying on A, B, C, D, and E. In fact, the whole point of tabs is to use names rather than single letters. To do this:

- Double click on tab indicator A.
- Type in October, and press the **Enter** key.
- Repeat this for the remaining tabs.

9.8 Adding a fourth dimension

This chapter has covered the idea of multiple sheets for the 12 different months. After one year has lapsed, the whole process really ought to start again. In this instance you would create another sheet on the lines of what has already been achieved. To do this easily, you could create a new Worksheet and copy the previous year's sheets into it.

The rest of this chapter now assumes that you have added a new month of January. This is now Sheet D, while the summary sheet is in Sheet E.

- Click on File, then Save As, and save the sheet as YEAR1.

- Repeat this but save the spreadsheet as YEAR2.

- Now open the YEAR1 sheet.

- Click on Window, then Tile, and you will see your two spreadsheets. (Both sheets are at present identical.)

- Click on a cell in YEAR1 and close the file. (You can double click on the minus sign in the bar to the left of YEAR1.WK4.)

- Click on YEAR2 and maximise the sheet so that it fills the screen. (Click on the upward-pointing black triangle in the bar to the right of YEAR2.WK4.)

- Position yourself in Sheet A (October).

To identify another spreadsheet in a formula you have to type <<FILENAME.WK4>> (in other words, two "less-than" and two "greater-than" symbols).

- Go through Sheets A, B and C in YEAR2.WK4 and alter the sales figures to anything you wish.

- Now type in the label Sales Change in cell A:E5 and on year in cell A:E6.

Screen dump 9.10 shows the result you will be aiming for where each month's figures are compared with the same month in the previous year.

The formula in cell E8 needs to subtract the value in YEAR1 cell A:B8 from the value in YEAR2 cell A:B8.

Type into cell A:E8 in file YEAR2.WK4 the formula:

+B8−<<YEAR1.WK4>>A:B8

THREE-DIMENSIONAL SPREADSHEETS

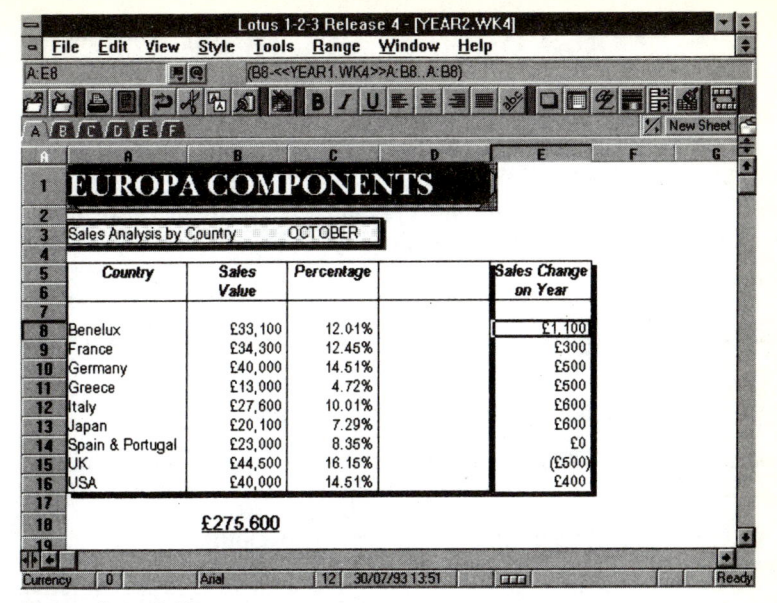

Screen dump 9.10

- Now copy this formula from cell E8 to cells E9..E16.

- Complete the formats of this new column for headings and currency.

The power of this should now be clear to see, where you can even copy the formula.

- Highlight cells E8 to E16 and copy them.

- Move to cell E8 in Sheet B.

- Paste the copied cells.

- Repeat this for the other sheets.

- Now save the current sheet as YEAR2.

- Finally, click on Print, click on All worksheets, and click on the OK button.

9.9 Chapter summary

In this chapter you have concentrated on creating and manipulating a three-dimensional spreadsheet. However, this has the advantage of leaving you with only one spreadsheet to concern yourself with in terms of file handling and presents you with easier formulae when working in three dimensions.

You have:

- created extra sheets in a spreadsheet to create a three-dimensional effect;
- viewed and moved between multiple sheets;
- set up the Group mode and performed Style set-ups for all sheets;
- typed data into one sheet and copied it to another;
- entered formulae and functions into a sheet that are derived from data in other sheets;
- opened another spreadsheet and worked with two multiple sheet spreadsheets;
- linked spreadsheets with the <<FILENAME>> facility.

10
– SAMPLE EXERCISES –

10.1 Aims of this chapter

This book has introduced you to a large variety of applications of spreadsheets. This chapter offers further ideas for spreadsheet use.

In addition, some exercises will help develop your skills further with Lotus 1-2-3 for Windows. If you work through the exercises in sequence, you will find that they become gradually more demanding.

10.2 Selling soft toys

1. Load your spreadsheet and type in the title EXPENSE DETAILS FOR HARRY'S SOFT TOYS on the first row. On the third row enter the author's name (yours) along with the date it is generated.
2. Generating today's date requires the @TODAY function followed by formatting the cell. (<u>S</u>tyle, <u>N</u>umber Format.)
3. Type in rows 6 to 11, as shown in **Screen dump 10.1**.
4. In cell A13 type in the label: TOTAL. (Right justify this by typing "TOTAL.)
5. Now type in a formula in cell B13 that calculates the sum of values in the range B7 to B11.
6. Copy the formula from cell B13 to cells C13 to E13.
7. In columns F and G type in data for MAY and JUNE:

	MAY	JUNE
WAGES	455	495
RENT	80	80
RATES	190	190
HEATING	15	18
SUNDRIES	26	33

8. In column H type in the heading: TOTAL.

9. In cell H7 type in a formula that totals the expenses for each category. Copy this formula from H7 to the range H8 to H11.

10. Copy the formula in cell E13 to cells F13 to H13.

11. Incorrect information has been collected on the costs of sundries, which should be 20 in February and 25 in April. Adjust the amounts accordingly to recalculate the total costs.

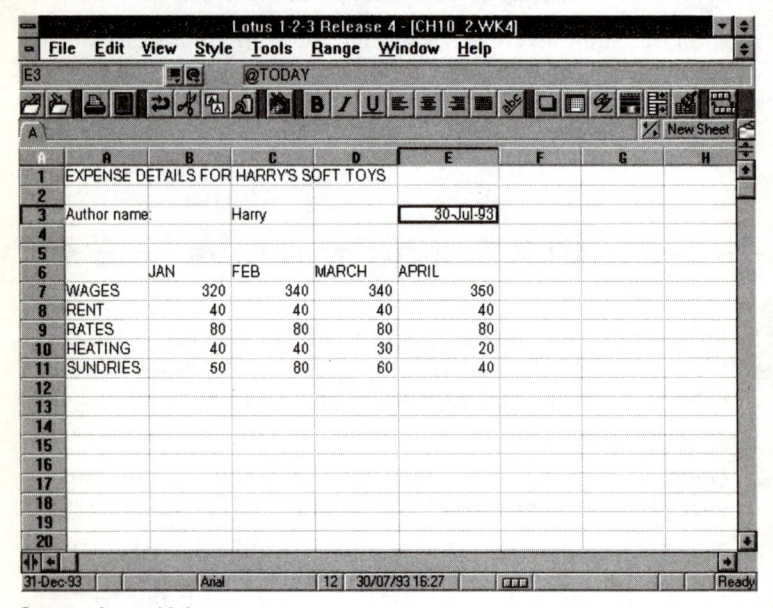

Screen dump 10.1

12. Format all numeric cells so that they are displayed in currency format to zero places of decimals.

SAMPLE EXERCISES

13. Add a new row at row 15. In cell A15 type in the title INCOME followed by the following sales income values for each month:

	JAN	FEB	MAR	APR	MAY	JUN
Sales Income	2,000	3,000	3,000	4,000	5,000	5,000

14. Now add a final row called SURPLUS and under the JAN column type in a formula that shows the surplus value as being: (Sales Income) minus (Total Cost). Copy this formula across the spreadsheet.

15. Check that all numeric formats are in currency and make any adjustments you feel necessary to tidy up the presentation of your spreadsheet.

16. Experiment with some of the fonts to improve the style of your spreadsheet.

17. Print the entire spreadsheet, remembering to define the range you want printed first.

18. Save your work under the file name HARRY.

10.3 Arnold's fish bar

1. Load your spreadsheet and type in your name and today's date at the top of the spreadsheet. Remember, the @TODAY function can be used for this, as described in Chapter 6.

2. Type in a title on row 3: ARNOLD'S FISH BAR SALES.

3. Widen column A.

4. Set up the spreadsheet with the labels shown in **Screen dump 10.2a**, with the column headings starting on row 5 and the row headings in column A.

5. The numbers that appear in the spreadsheet should also be typed in. Make sure that text is left justified and numbers right justified.

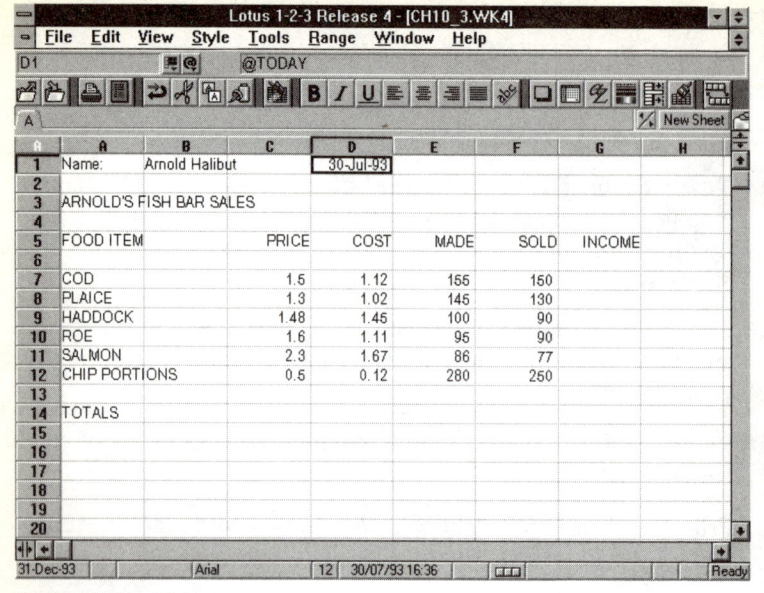

Screen dump 10.2a

	A	B	C	D	E	F	G
1	Name:	Arnold Halibut		30-Jul-93			
2							
3	ARNOLD'S FISH BAR SALES						
4							
5	FOOD ITEM		PRICE	COST	MADE	SOLD	INCOME
6							
7	COD		1.5	1.12	155	150	
8	PLAICE		1.3	1.02	145	130	
9	HADDOCK		1.48	1.45	100	90	
10	ROE		1.6	1.11	95	90	
11	SALMON		2.3	1.67	86	77	
12	CHIP PORTIONS		0.5	0.12	280	250	
13							
14	TOTALS						

6. Generate the INCOME obtained from COD by multiplying the PRICE by the number SOLD and putting the answer in the INCOME column.

7. On row 14 use a formula to calculate the total items MADE, the total dishes SOLD, and the total INCOME.

8. Add an extra column to the spreadsheet to show the profit made on each dish. Under the heading PROFIT generate the data for each dish using the formula:

   PROFIT = INCOME − (COST * MADE)

9. Format all money values to currency.

10. Now change the numeric data to the ones shown in **Screen dump 10.2b** to check that your spreadsheet still calculates the INCOME, PROFIT and TOTALS correctly with the new figures.

11. Produce two more columns with the column headings UNSOLD to hold the column of stock for each item that was left unsold (MADE-SOLD), and a column headed WASTE to hold the cost to the fish bar of this unsold stock (UNSOLD * COST).

SAMPLE EXERCISES

A	B	C	D	E	F	G	H	I
Name:	Arnold Halibut	30-Jul-93						
ARNOLD'S FISH BAR SALES								
FOOD ITEM	PRICE	COST	MADE	SOLD	INCOME	PROFIT	UNSOLD	WASTE
COD	£1.50	£1.12	155	150	£225.00	£51.40	5	£5.60
PLAICE	£1.30	£1.02	145	130	£169.00	£21.10	15	£15.30
HADDOCK	£1.48	£1.45	100	90	£133.20	(£11.80)	10	£14.50
ROE	£1.60	£1.11	95	90	£144.00	£38.55	5	£5.55
SALMON	£2.30	£1.67	86	77	£177.10	£33.48	9	£15.03
CHIP PORTIONS	£0.50	£0.12	280	250	£125.00	£91.40	30	£3.60
TOTALS			861	787	£973.30	£224.13		£59.58

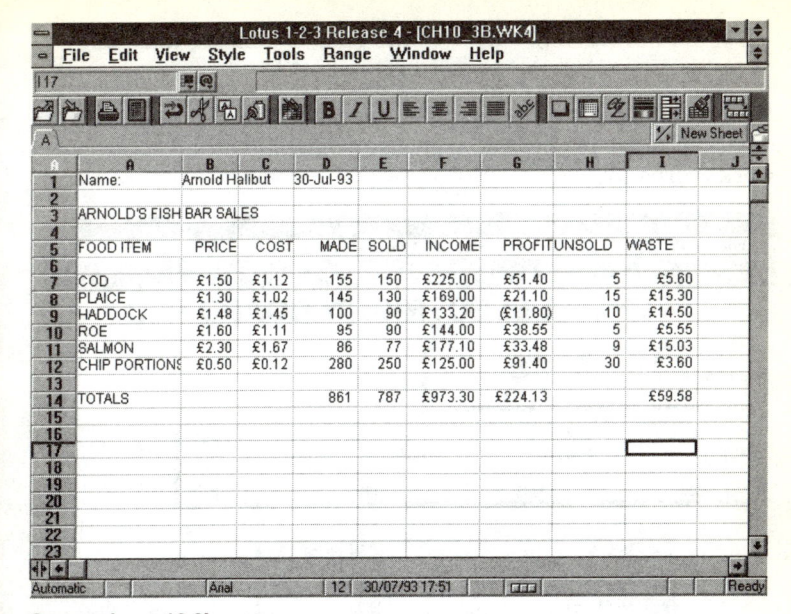

Screen dump 10.2b

12. Zoom out so that all data are in view on your screen and then compare the outcome with that shown in **Screen dump 10.2b**.

13. Make any alterations to the presentation required and save your spreadsheet.

14. Print out this spreadsheet.

10.4 An electricity bill

This exercise requires you to set up a model electricity bill similar to that shown in **Screen dump 10.3**. If you have an electricity bill of your own to use, then model it around this instead.

When you set out this spreadsheet, bear in mind the following formulae:

- No. of units = (Current meter reading) − (Last meter reading)
- Total Cost for units in £ = (No. of Units) * (Cost per Unit in pence) / 100
- VAT = (VAT Rate) * (Total Cost for Units + Standing Charge)

- TOTAL NOW DUE = (Total Cost for Units) + (Standing Charge) + VAT

When you complete the exercise, experiment with a few bills with different meter readings to convince yourself that the spreadsheet works correctly.

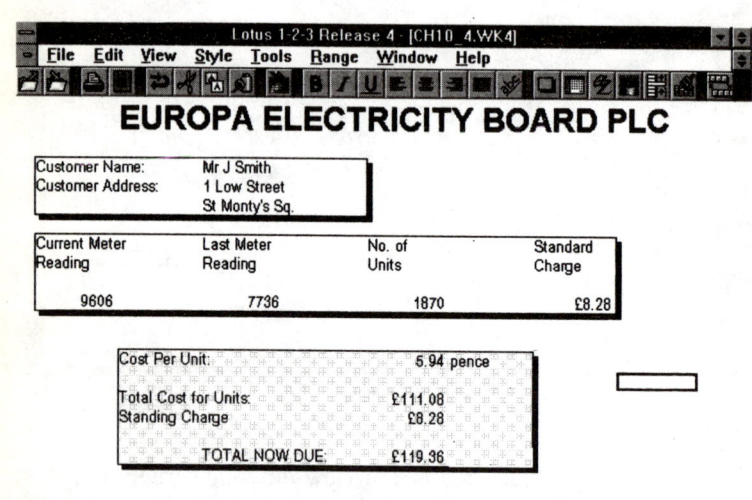

EUROPA ELECTRICITY BOARD PLC

Customer Name:	Mr J Smith
Customer Address:	1 Low Street
	St Monty's Sq.

Current Meter Reading	Last Meter Reading	No. of Units	Standard Charge
9606	7736	1870	£8.28

Cost Per Unit:	5.94 pence
Total Cost for Units:	£111.08
Standing Charge	£8.28
TOTAL NOW DUE:	£119.36

Screen dump 10.3

10.5 Calorie control

The following exercise is an example of how a spreadsheet can be used to give instant and accurate measures of the number of calories contained within a specific diet. When working through it, you ought to consider how it can be extended to include other variables such as certain vitamins.

The spreadsheet is split up into two parts: one part contains the ACTUAL DIET of a given patient, while the second part contains the CALORIE CONTROL CHART. Basically, the spreadsheet will collect the details of the patient from a user and then calculate the calories consumed in the diet by reading these details from the Calorie Control Chart.

SAMPLE EXERCISES

Calorie control chart

The chart will need to go somewhere on the spreadsheet where it is out of the way, as this data will be standard and does not need to be changed too often. Ideally, create a second sheet B.

1. Insert one Sheet after the current one. Make sure you are working in Sheet B.

2. Turn the Group mode off because you will not want formats and column widths to be the same throughout.

3. Start at cell position B:A1 and type in the details as shown in **Screen dump 10.4a** which will hold the calorie content per 100 grams of a range of food and drink.

When generating this table, you will need to adjust the column widths to fit the data.

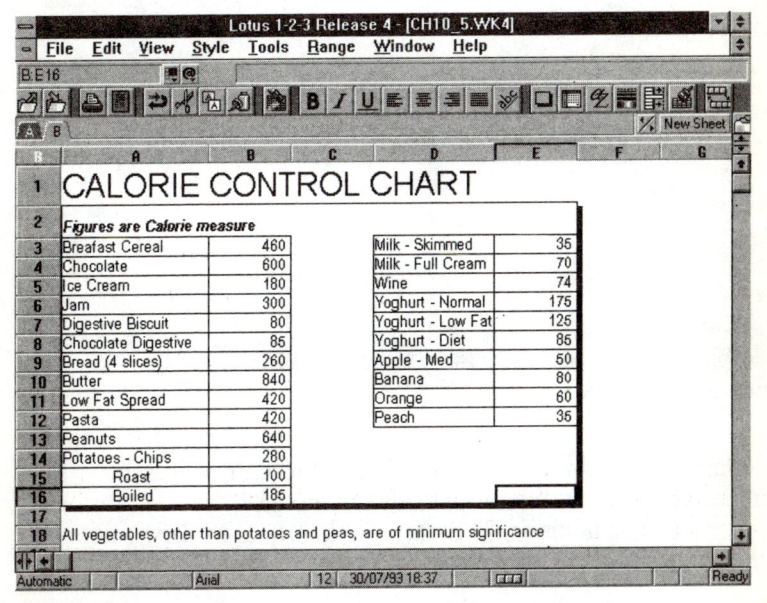

CALORIE CONTROL CHART

Figures are Calorie measure

A	B		C	D
Breafast Cereal	460		Milk - Skimmed	35
Chocolate	600		Milk - Full Cream	70
Ice Cream	180		Wine	74
Jam	300		Yoghurt - Normal	175
Digestive Biscuit	80		Yoghurt - Low Fat	125
Chocolate Digestive	85		Yoghurt - Diet	85
Bread (4 slices)	260		Apple - Med	50
Butter	840		Banana	80
Low Fat Spread	420		Orange	60
Pasta	420		Peach	35
Peanuts	640			
Potatoes - Chips	280			
Roast	100			
Boiled	185			

All vegetables, other than potatoes and peas, are of minimum significance

Screen dump 10.4a

4. Change the look of the sheet. (Remove grid lines, add a border, colour, etc.)

5. Print out the chart. (You will need to specify the range you want printed prior to its actual printing.)

Patient Diet sheet

6. Return to Sheet A (**Screen dump 10.4b**).

7. Type in a patient diet sheet for a given day, starting at position A1, something like that set out in **Screen dumps 10.4b and 10.4c**. You will observe that the spreadsheet exceeds the number of lines in one screen. You can, of course Zoom Out to fit it all onto one screen, but it will be very hard to read.

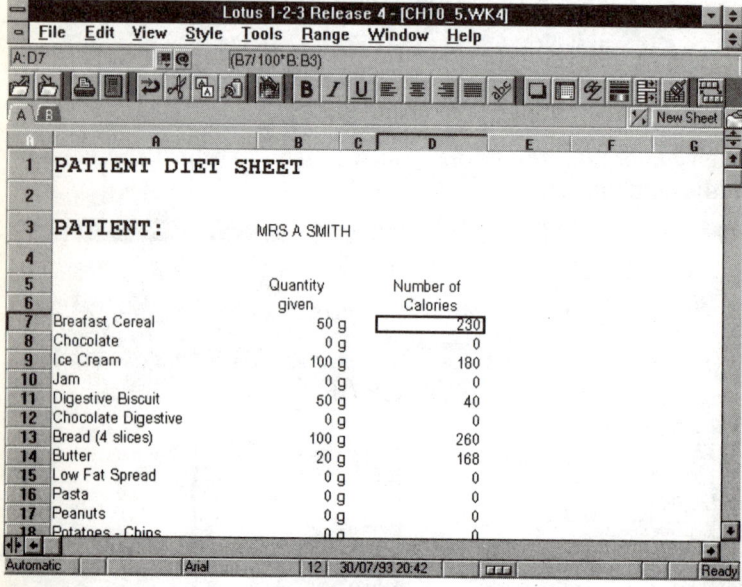

	A	B	C	D
1	PATIENT DIET SHEET			
2				
3	PATIENT:		MRS A SMITH	
4				
5		Quantity		Number of
6		given		Calories
7	Breafast Cereal	50 g		230
8	Chocolate	0 g		0
9	Ice Cream	100 g		180
10	Jam	0 g		0
11	Digestive Biscuit	50 g		40
12	Chocolate Digestive	0 g		0
13	Bread (4 slices)	100 g		260
14	Butter	20 g		168
15	Low Fat Spread	0 g		0
16	Pasta	0 g		0
17	Peanuts	0 g		0
18	Potatoes - Chips	0 g		0

Cell: A:D7, Contents: (B7/100*B.B3)

Screen dump 10.4b

Column C has been used to indicate the unit of measure. It is important that you do not put this in column B, as it would make the values non-numeric. The effect is, therefore, to allow you to use the quantities to perform some calculations with.

SAMPLE EXERCISES

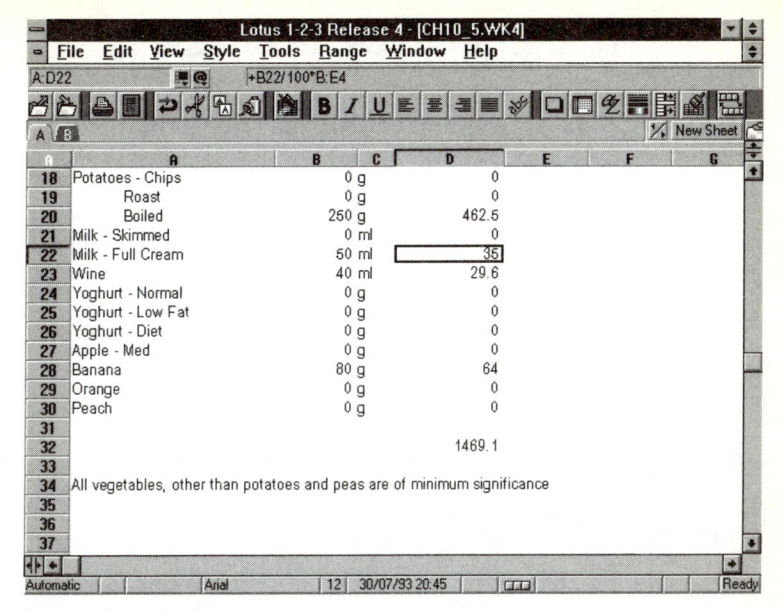

```
                Lotus 1-2-3 Release 4 - [CH10_5.WK4]
   File  Edit  View  Style  Tools  Range  Window  Help
A:D22              +B22/100*B:E4
```

	A	B	C	D	E	F	G
18	Potatoes - Chips	0 g		0			
19	Roast	0 g		0			
20	Boiled	250 g		462.5			
21	Milk - Skimmed	0 ml		0			
22	Milk - Full Cream	50 ml		35			
23	Wine	40 ml		29.6			
24	Yoghurt - Normal	0 g		0			
25	Yoghurt - Low Fat	0 g		0			
26	Yoghurt - Diet	0 g		0			
27	Apple - Med	0 g		0			
28	Banana	80 g		64			
29	Orange	0 g		0			
30	Peach	0 g		0			
31							
32				1469.1			
33							
34	All vegetables, other than potatoes and peas are of minimum significance

Screen dump 10.4c

8. Be careful to create a column C for the unit of measure (g or ml) and narrow the column. Only the number can go into the amounts given in column B.

9. Make sure that the entries of the NUMBER OF CALORIES are found and calculated by the computer. For example, the number for Full Cream Milk in cell location D22 is calculated as follows: Grams given, to be found in cell B22, divided by 100 and then multiplied by the number of calories per 100 millilitres which was placed into cell E4 of Sheet B. Consequently, for cell D22 the formula will need to read: +B22/100*B:E4.

10. Perform some of the finishing touches to improve the presentation of your work.

11. Finally, use the @SUM function to find the totals for this patient, then print the details of the patient's diet.

10.6 Employee sickness

This exercise requires you to perform the following tasks:

1. Ensure you have started with a blank spreadsheet.
2. Type in a heading and a list of employee names, as shown in **Screen dump 10.5**.
3. Type in for each employee: the number of days sickness and the number of possible days they could have worked.
4. Type in dates From and To using the @DATE function.
5. Calculate the number of days between the two dates.

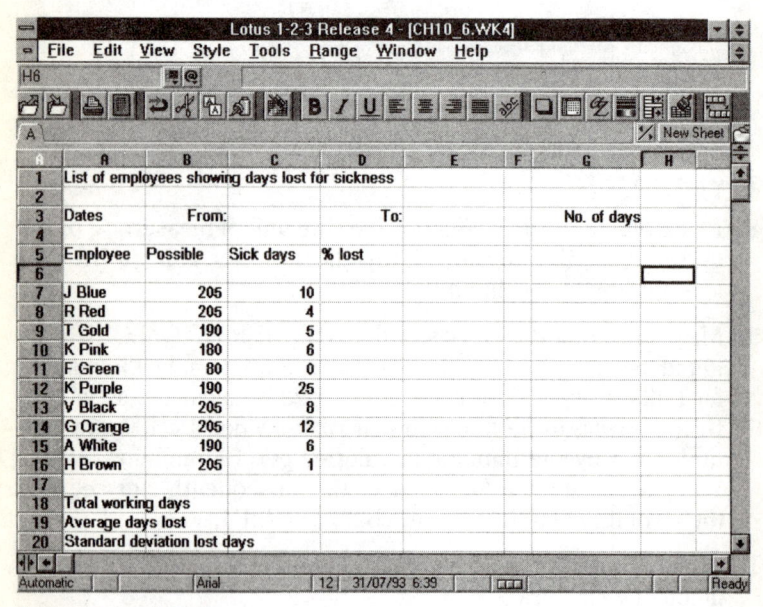

	A	B	C	D	E	F	G	H
1	List of employees showing days lost for sickness							
2								
3	Dates	From:		To:			No. of days	
4								
5	Employee	Possible	Sick days	% lost				
6								
7	J Blue	205	10					
8	R Red	205	4					
9	T Gold	190	5					
10	K Pink	180	6					
11	F Green	80	0					
12	K Purple	190	25					
13	V Black	205	8					
14	G Orange	205	12					
15	A White	190	6					
16	H Brown	205	1					
17								
18	Total working days							
19	Average days lost							
20	Standard deviation lost days							

Screen dump 10.5

6. Calculate the percentage of days lost through sickness for each employee.
7. Now create NAMED ranges: possible, days lost, and percentage for columns B, C, and D respectively. Paste a table of the named ranges similar to that shown in **Screen dump 10.5**.

SAMPLE EXERCISES

8. Calculate: total working days, total lost days, an average percentage of days' sickness, and a standard deviation for sickness days.

Note: In order to tackle this Lotus 1-2-3 has an in-built function for the standard deviation: @STD (Percentage).

9. Smarten up the presentation.
10. Get a printout of the table you have generated.
11. Alter some of the sick days' figures and possible work days, to make sure that the calculations work. Print out a second spreadsheet.

10.7 Price lists for a transport company

Examine **Screen dump 10.6**, showing a transport company's price list, before starting this exercise.

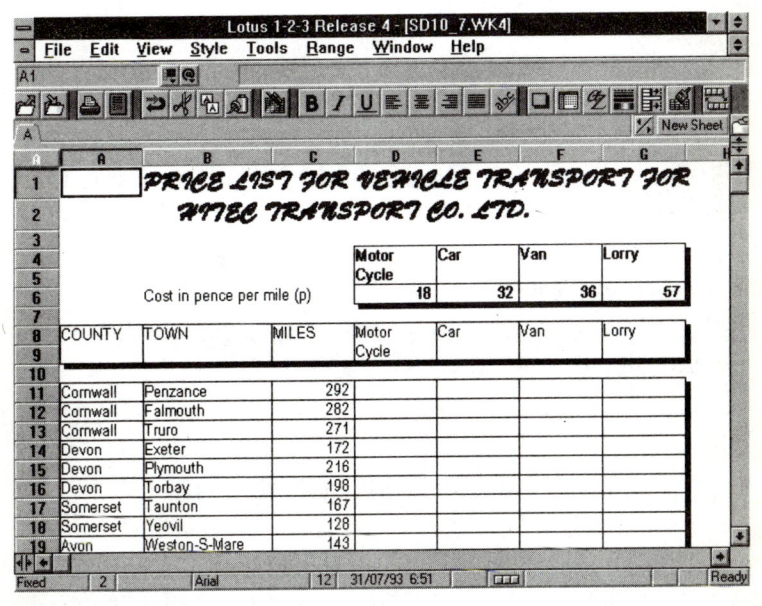

A	B	C	D	E	F	G
	PRICE LIST FOR VEHICLE TRANSPORT FOR HITEC TRANSPORT CO. LTD.					
			Motor Cycle	Car	Van	Lorry
	Cost in pence per mile (p)		18	32	36	57
COUNTY	TOWN	MILES	Motor Cycle	Car	Van	Lorry
Cornwall	Penzance	292				
Cornwall	Falmouth	282				
Cornwall	Truro	271				
Devon	Exeter	172				
Devon	Plymouth	216				
Devon	Torbay	198				
Somerset	Taunton	167				
Somerset	Yeovil	128				
Avon	Weston-S-Mare	143				

Screen dump 10.6

From observation you will see that there is a heading for county and a town or city within that county. The mileage indicates the number of miles from the town to a fictitious London Office.

The costs indicate the cost per mile for running each vehicle type. For each town, therefore, the cost of running a vehicle from London to the stated town is calculated. The use of such a spreadsheet allows a new price list to be easily and quickly constructed each time the prices per mile change.

1. Construct such a list for England, Scotland, Wales or any other country by having every county (or province or state) represented by between two and four principal towns or cities. You will need a map of the country with the mileage between the town or city and your chosen central location.

2. For each country, produce two lists with the following costs:

	first list	second list
Motor Cycle:	£0.18	£0.21
Car:	£0.32	£0.34
Van:	£0.36	£0.33
Truck:	£0.57	£0.55

The monetary values should be in currency format.

3. Rearrange your list using the Database Sort facilities into County (or Province or State) order and, within each county, organised in town or city order.

4. Save what you created in task 3 and produce the list in town order.

5. Repeat task 4 but rearrange the list into order of distance, with the farthest distance at the top of the list.

   (The whole width of the spreadsheet can be made visible on the screen by adjusting the column widths.)

10.8 World weather chart

This spreadsheet sets out a world weather chart to show the temperature in different locations throughout the world. See **Screen dump 10.7**.

SAMPLE EXERCISES

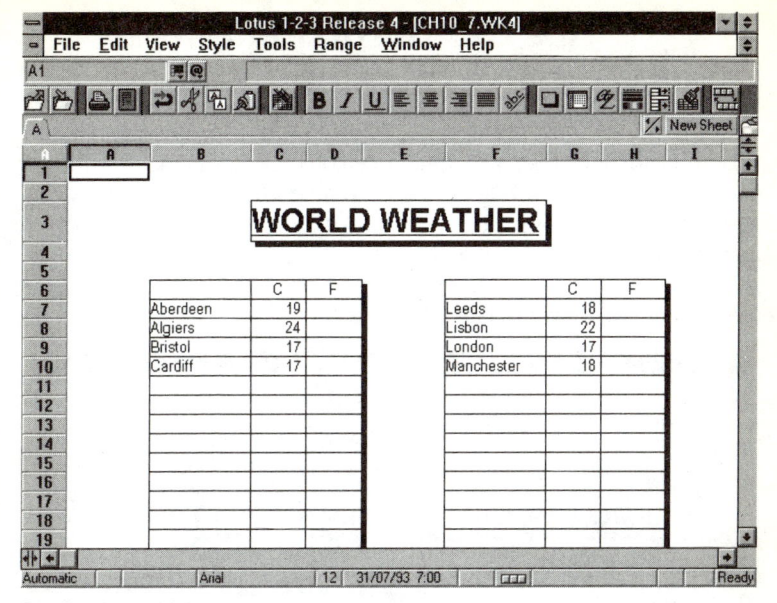

Screen dump 10.7

1. Design a spreadsheet to display this information. Include data taken from newspapers. The temperature in Fahrenheit should be calculated from the temperature in Centigrade by using the formula: Fahrenheit = Centigrade x 1.8 + 32.

2. At the foot of your table, show:

   the average temperature
   the number of locations
   the name of the hottest place
   the name of the coldest place

   These figures should be determined using the Lotus 1-2-3 functions.

3. Print the table.

4. Alter the temperatures.

10.9 Car burglar alarm explosion

This spreadsheet requires you to set out the components of a car burglar alarm system that is to be produced by a small engineering company. The final product will be in black-box form, ready to install in a car. The objective of this exercise is to calculate, at component level, the cost of materials and production of the alarm in order to derive a profitable selling-price.

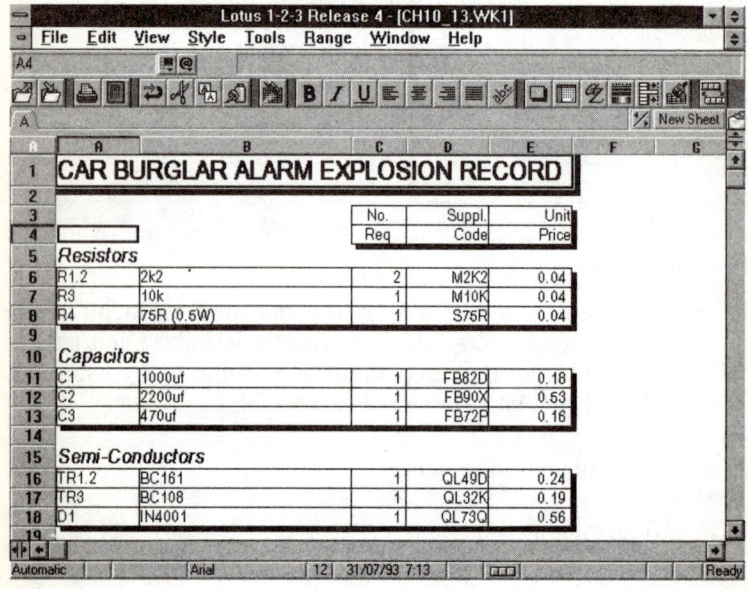

	A	B	C	D	E
1	CAR BURGLAR ALARM EXPLOSION RECORD				
2					
3			No. Req	Suppl. Code	Unit Price
4					
5	*Resistors*				
6	R1.2	2k2	2	M2K2	0.04
7	R3	10k	1	M10K	0.04
8	R4	75R (0.5W)	1	S75R	0.04
9					
10	*Capacitors*				
11	C1	1000uf	1	FB82D	0.18
12	C2	2200uf	1	FB90X	0.53
13	C3	470uf	1	FB72P	0.16
14					
15	*Semi-Conductors*				
16	TR1.2	BC161	1	QL49D	0.24
17	TR3	BC108	1	QL32K	0.19
18	D1	IN4001	1	QL73Q	0.56

Screen dump 10.8a

From the list, shown in **Screen dump 10.8a** and **Screen dump 10.8b**, you should be able to enter the number of alarm systems you wish to make. The spreadsheet will then produce a "shopping list", giving a list of the components needed and their costs along with a total cost. It is suggested, therefore, that your spreadsheet has the following sections:

- A component breakdown, as shown in **Screen dump 10.8a**.

- A column to hold costs of multiple components; for example $10 \times 0.4W$ metal film 2K2.

SAMPLE EXERCISES

- An entry for the desired number of "final product" car alarm(s).
- A list of total components needed, with unit costs, in alphabetical order.

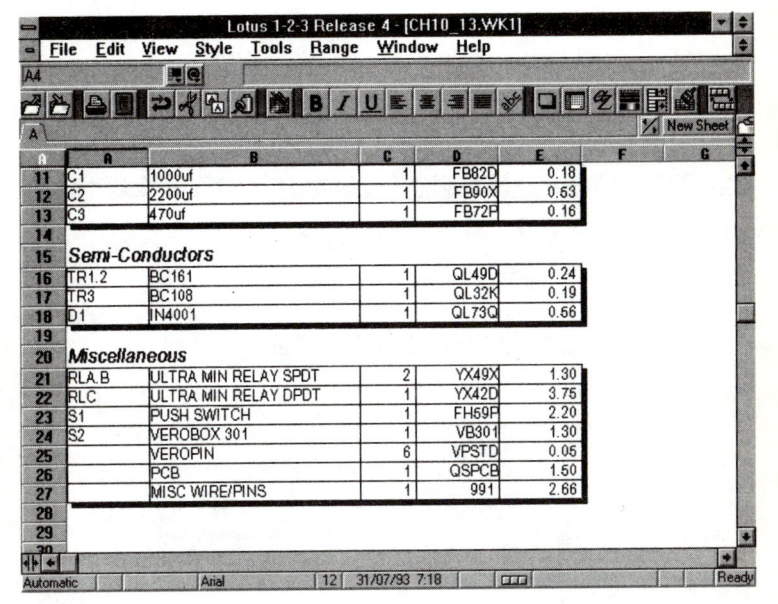

	A	B	C	D	E
11	C1	1000uf	1	FB82D	0.18
12	C2	2200uf	1	FB90X	0.53
13	C3	470uf	1	FB72R	0.16
14					
15	*Semi-Conductors*				
16	TR1.2	BC161	1	QL49D	0.24
17	TR3	BC108	1	QL32K	0.19
18	D1	IN4001	1	QL73Q	0.66
19					
20	*Miscellaneous*				
21	RLA.B	ULTRA MIN RELAY SPDT	2	YX49X	1.30
22	RLC	ULTRA MIN RELAY DPDT	1	YX42D	3.75
23	S1	PUSH SWITCH	1	FH59F	2.20
24	S2	VEROBOX 301	1	VB301	1.30
25		VEROPIN	6	VPSTD	0.05
26		PCB	1	QSPCB	1.50
27		MISC WIRE/PINS	1	991	2.66

Screen dump 10.8b

Try taking advantage of macros in order to sort the list by costs as well as in component order. Also, use a macro to simplify the printing of each section.

You will find the use of a horizontal window valuable because the spreadsheet has more rows of information than can be seen on the screen at any one time.

10.10 League tables

This spreadsheet is designed to show a football league championship table, and can easily be adapted to suit any league-based sport. The table has been sorted so that the club with the highest number of points appears at the top. When two clubs have the same number of points, the order is by goal difference.

Part of the table takes the form of the one shown in **Screen dump 10.9**.

The points system assumed is:

Win = 3 points
Draw = 1 point

Games Played = Won + Lost + Drawn
Goal Difference = (goals for) − (goals against)

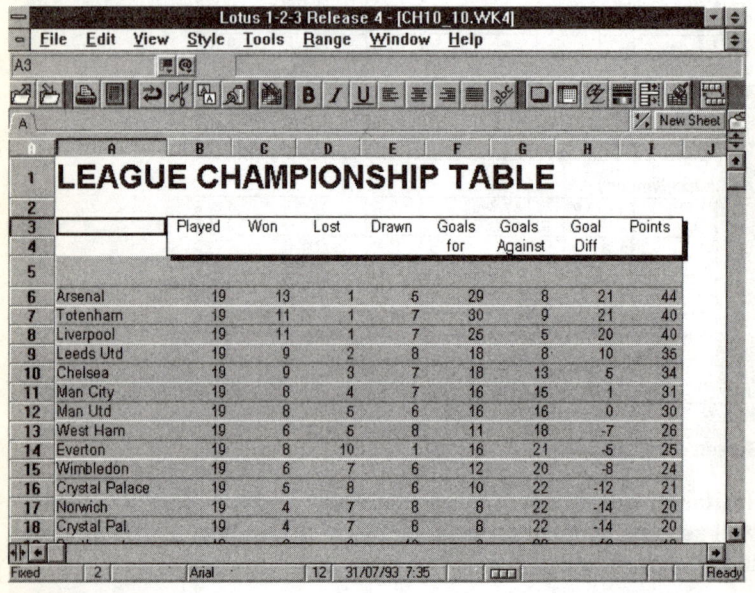

	Played	Won	Lost	Drawn	Goals for	Goals Against	Goal Diff	Points
LEAGUE CHAMPIONSHIP TABLE								
Arsenal	19	13	1	5	29	8	21	44
Totenham	19	11	1	7	30	9	21	40
Liverpool	19	11	1	7	26	5	20	40
Leeds Utd	19	9	2	8	18	8	10	35
Chelsea	19	9	3	7	18	13	5	34
Man City	19	8	4	7	16	15	1	31
Man Utd	19	8	5	6	16	16	0	30
West Ham	19	6	5	8	11	18	-7	26
Everton	19	8	10	1	16	21	-5	25
Wimbledon	19	6	7	6	12	20	-8	24
Crystal Palace	19	5	8	6	10	22	-12	21
Norwich	19	4	7	8	8	22	-14	20
Crystal Pal.	19	4	7	8	8	22	-14	20

Screen dump 10.9

1. Produce a spreadsheet for this table. You could take details from a league table listed in the sports section of a newspaper.

2. At the foot of the table show the following:

   Number of clubs
   Highest number of wins
   Highest number of defeats
   Average number of goals for
   Average number of goals against
   The average goal difference

   All these figures should be shown to the nearest whole figure.

SAMPLE EXERCISES

10.11 Hayley computer services

This problem involves the setting up of a simple cash budget depicting a cash flow for a company. The pro-forma set out in **Screen dump 10.10** is designed to help you get started with the problem.

Hayley Computer Services Ltd is a small company offering computer consultancy and professional training to small businesses. The company has been trading for two years, the only staff being Mr James and his wife. Mr James is now worried that the £5,000 overdraft facility granted by his bank will be insufficient to finance his company's modest expansion. To assist in his investigation of several possible plans, he has decided to set up a cash flow model covering the next 12 months.

Mrs James has made the following estimates for the year ending December 31:

- Fees received by the company in January will be £2,900 and these will rise steadily by 5% per month.

Expenses of the company are expected to be:

- Rental of premises at £400 per month, fixed at this amount for the year.

- General expenses of £500 in January, rising steadily by 3% a month.

- Fixed motor vehicle expenses of £120 per month.

- Wages and PAYE tax deductions of £1,800 a month, fixed for 6 months, but increased from July onwards by 25%.

In March Mr James intends changing his company car. He believes that he will be able to sell his present car for £5,600 and that the replacement will cost £7,900.

In September he expects to pay tax of £5,920 on the company's previous year's profits.

On 1 January the company's bank account is expected to be overdrawn by £3,100.

LOTUS 1–2–3 WINDOWS

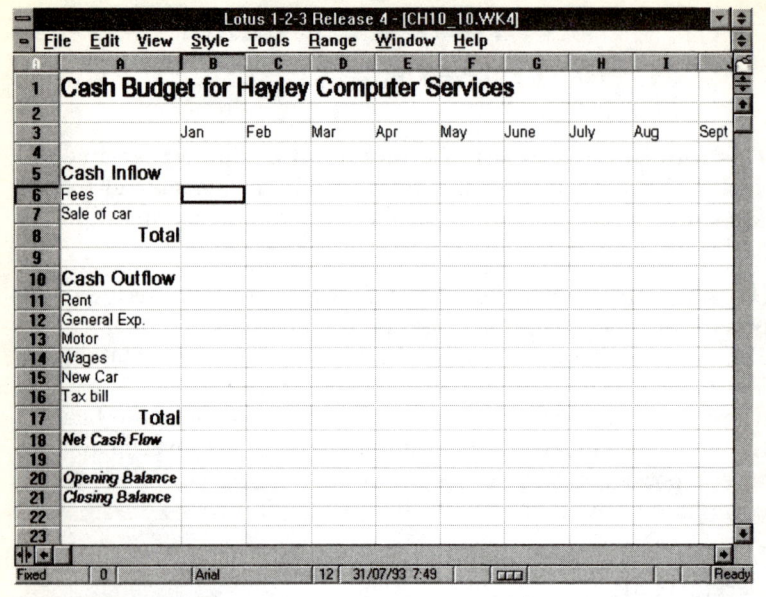

	A	B	C	D	E	F	G	H	I
1	**Cash Budget for Hayley Computer Services**								
2									
3		Jan	Feb	Mar	Apr	May	June	July	Aug	Sept
4									
5	**Cash Inflow**								
6	Fees								
7	Sale of car								
8	Total								
9									
10	**Cash Outflow**								
11	Rent								
12	General Exp.								
13	Motor								
14	Wages								
15	New Car								
16	Tax bill								
17	Total								
18	*Net Cash Flow*								
19									
20	*Opening Balance*								
21	*Closing Balance*								

Screen dump 10.10

1. Set up the model of the company's cash flow for the 12 months to December. You have the pro-forma set out in **Screen dump 10.11** to help you get started. All figures should be displayed to the nearest whole figure.

2. By modifying the basic model, ascertain the effect of each of the following proposals in turn on the company's overdraft position, so that Mr James can decide which option most favours his bank balance:

   (a) A new issue of shares to Mr James's uncle, giving a cash inflow of £4,500 in February.

   (b) Taking out a loan of £4,000 in January to be repaid in December with interest of £450.

   (c) Deferring the purchase of the new car for 12 months but facing extra running expenses of £40 a month after March.

   (d) Paying £1,000 for advertising in January with an increase in sales of £250 a month (over and above the 5% growth) beginning in February. Also, vacating his rented premises and working at home from January.

SAMPLE EXERCISES

10.12 The rapid cook microwave company

This problem requires you to design a cash budget similar to that of exercise 10.11. However, the problems are more demanding and you are given less help with the initial layout.

A group of partners are to set up a limited company for the purpose of manufacturing and selling microwave ovens, with a start-up Share Capital of £60,000 in the bank on 1 June and an anticipated injection of further Share Capital from new shareholders once the business is underway.

The plans for the company are as follows:

- It will produce 120 ovens a month starting in June, but expects sales to start from 60 in July, increasing in steps of 20 each month until they reach 140 per month.

- The ovens will sell for £320 each with customer accounts being settled in the second month after the month of purchase.

- The overheads will be fixed at £5,000 per month, paid one month in arrears.

- In September the business will pay £150,000 for machinery and computers needed to start up the business.

- In November an extra injection of capital is expected. This amount should be £75,000.

- The unit (variable) production costs, which are not expected to rise in the period under review, will be as follows:

    Materials   £90
    Labour   £80
    Variable Overheads £40

    Materials will be bought as needed with payments one month later. Labour will have to be paid in the month in which the expense is incurred, as will variable overheads.

- Interest on the previous month's overdraft is to be charged at 1.5% plus a £10 standing charge by the bank.

In order to satisfy the bank manager that the request for additional funding of the business with an overdraft is reasonable, the business has been asked to draw up a cash flow forecast for the first 7 months of operations from June to December.

- Use Lotus 1-2-3 to create the cash flow table that the bank manager wants to see before granting the overdraft provisions requested. The cash flow table will also need to show size of overdraft required.

- You should produce not only the print-out of the table as seen on the screen, but also a print-out showing the formulae used, in case the bank manager questions the derivation of the figures.

In October, the business finds that it is proceeding very much as had been planned and that advance orders suggest that sales are likely to rise to 150 from January, falling to 130 from April. This is extremely encouraging, but leaves the business with the problem of how it is going to be able to satisfy demand.

Production capacity of 120 ovens a month has been sufficient to cope with demand thus far, but...

Overtime working, which will inevitably increase labour costs, seems to be called for and the business is to consider how this can be organised. The directors have already talked to staff and sufficient staff have said they would be willing to work overtime.

It is estimated that when production rises above 120 per month each microwave will add £40 to labour costs. Also, while the factory is working overtime, overheads will rise to £5,800 per month. New machinery and maintenance costs of £12,000 will have to be paid for in April.

- Use your existing spreadsheet model as a starting-point and modify accordingly. Extend the cash budget to June, investigating some of the possibilities. You may assume that only labour costs and additional overheads will be affected by the overtime working, and you should remember that selling microwaves that have not yet been produced is *not* an acceptable means of improving cash flow.

- In order that you have a record of the consequences of the alternative strategies you have investigated, you should print copies of the spreadsheets with sub-headings which indicate what strategy you were examining.

SAMPLE EXERCISES

10.13 Council house survey

On examination of the sample spreadsheet in **Screen dump 10.11**, it should be evident what is required from the survey in terms of the initial data.

The aim is to show in graphical form the types of housing stock that exist within this fictitious borough and the number of people living in the houses.

From the spreadsheet you are to extract a number of bar graphs (or pie charts) showing the distribution of the total housing among the various groups and the number of occupants in each type of accommodation. You will be able to produce a large number of useful charts from such figures.

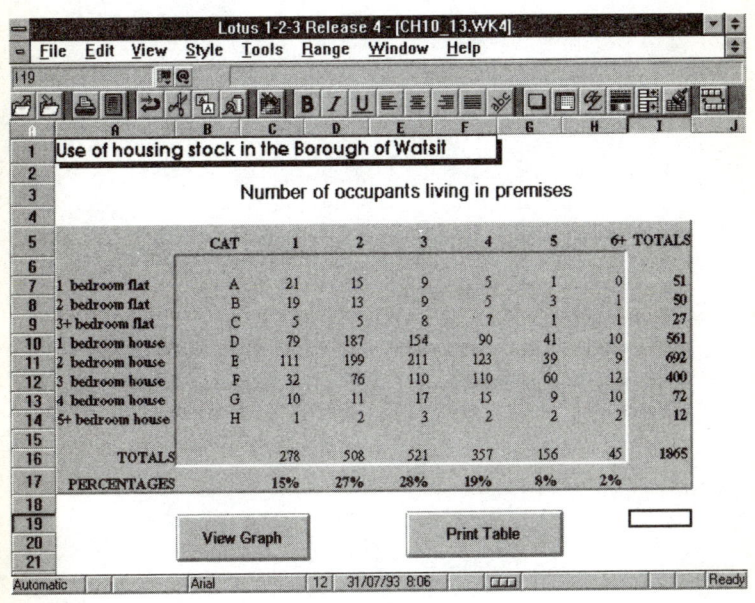

	CAT	1	2	3	4	5	6+	TOTALS
1 bedroom flat	A	21	15	9	5	1	0	51
2 bedroom flat	B	19	13	9	5	3	1	50
3+ bedroom flat	C	5	5	8	7	1	1	27
1 bedroom house	D	79	187	154	90	41	10	561
2 bedroom house	E	111	199	211	123	39	9	692
3 bedroom house	F	32	76	110	110	60	12	400
4 bedroom house	G	10	11	17	15	9	10	72
5+ bedroom house	H	1	2	3	2	2	2	12
TOTALS		278	508	521	357	156	45	1865
PERCENTAGES		15%	27%	28%	19%	8%	2%	

Use of housing stock in the Borough of Watsit — Number of occupants living in premises

Screen dump 10.11

Produce a number of such charts displaying different aspects of data, so that someone else can understand the data quickly and easily without having to read through the table.

When setting up a bar chart or pie chart, one of the problems you will soon face is avoiding too much congestion on the screen.

As a finishing touch, create two macros, one to print the table and the other to view the graph. If you are a Release 4 user, assign these two macros to buttons in order to simplify the process for a user.

GLOSSARY

Abort The action of stopping the execution of a program while it is still running. If you are in the middle of updating a record, for example, you may need to abort to avoid a serious error. In Lotus 1-2-3 this is usually done by pressing the **Esc** key.

Absolute reference In a formula, a reference to a cell that does not change when you copy the formula. An absolute reference always refers to the same cell or range. To create an absolute cell reference, enter a $ (dollar sign) before the worksheet letter, column letter, and row number ($A:$A$4) when you write the formula. To create an absolute range name, enter a $ (dollar sign) before the range name ($INTEREST). For example, if you copy the formula +$A$1*B10 entered in cell C10 to C11 and C12, the formula changes to +$A$1*B11 and +$A$1*B12. The absolute reference ($A$1) does not change.

Access Referring to data stored in a file. For example, disk access is needed if a Sales Ledger activity is to keep customer records updated.

Algorithm A series of instructions set up in logical order and designed to perform an activity such as sorting stock records into stock number order. The algorithm will be capable of being converted into a computer program.

Amend Changing a record in a file. For example, altering a customer's address in a database is a form of file amendment. The term can also be applied to altering the details of a spreadsheet file in order to update a set of figures.

Analyst A person who has the job of analysing various activities, for example, systems analyst, database analyst, cost analyst. With respect to the systems analyst, such people are often concerned with analysing computer-based information systems or manual system with a view to computerising them. The use of spreadsheets may be one of many applications an analyst will consider.

Annotating The process of creating and editing objects such as polygons, text boxes and rectangles. Such annotated objects can be created in a chart and subsequently added to spreadsheets and graphs.

Append Adding new records to a database table.

Application A specific use to which a computer is put, e.g. spreadsheet, payroll, sales, job costing. Such applications are often performed on a computer by a software package, or part of an integrated software package.

Arrow keys (pointer-movement keys) Keys that control the movement of the cell pointer, menu pointer, and insertion point. These keys include UP, DOWN, LEFT, RIGHT, PG UP, PG DN, and HOME, and can be combined with CTRL and END to move around spreadsheets in the same file and other active files.

@ functions Built-in formulas that will perform specialised calculations automatically. For example, @SUM (range) adds all numbers in the specified range. Lotus 1-2-3 has a large number of such functions covering many specialist areas as well as the more general ones.

Background printing A process whereby the computer prints a document while continuing to allow an operator to use the computer or computer terminal to process data. One of the benefits of working in a Windows environment is that background printing is now common practice.

Backing storage Often referred to as secondary storage, it allows data to be stored on media such as disks for longterm storage purposes, i.e. off-line data storage.

Backup A process of copying all data from one source to another for safe keeping. This option is offered by Lotus 1-2-3 when you attempt to save a file that already has a file with that name.

Borders These are the column letters and row numbers around the spreadsheet area that identify cell locations.

Buffer A part of memory used as a temporary store to hold data from an input device. For example, most printers have a buffer memory for storing data prior to printing it. Also, keyboards often hold at least one line of data before it is sent to the computer's processor.

Bug An error in a program.

Bus A means of communication channel which data travel along. Such channels consist of a control bus, data bus, address bus and peripheral bus.

Button (Macro) A small button-like object on the screen that, when clicked on with a mouse, runs a macro.

Byte A measure of computer memory, normally containing 8 single bits. Each byte often represents a single character. 1024 of these bytes is referred to as a Kilobyte.

Cache memory A form of buffer memory that works at high speed and is capable of keeping up with a computer's CPU. It acts as a buffer between the CPU and the slower main memory. Because the CPU is not delayed by memory access, processing is speeded up. The operating system will load segments of programs into cache memory from disks.

Carriage return A single character sent to the computer by pressing the **Return** or **Enter** key on the keyboard. Such carriage returns are often used to release data from the keyboard buffer to the computer's processor.

Cascading windows This shows different windows one behind the other. Cascading spreadsheets will give the image of spreadsheets piled up. You will have to have more than one spreadsheet open at any time to get the benefit of this.

Cell The basic unit of a Lotus 1-2-3 worksheet. The intersection of a column and a row forms a cell. You enter and store data in a cell.

Central processing unit Often referred to as the processor or microprocessor and the main unit of any computer system. The processor accepts its data from input devices, processes the data and sends it to output devices such as screens and printers, or to a disk for saving.

Character A single element in coded form for the processor, such as a letter or a single number digit. Such characters are normally 8 bits, or one byte, long.

Classic 1-2-3 Classic is the command menu of Lotus 1-2-3 for DOS Release 3.1, available in Lotus 1-2-3 Release 4. To use 1-2-3 Classic: press / (slash) or < (less-than symbol).

Click To press the mouse button and quickly release it.

Clipboard A storage area Windows uses to temporarily store data when you use Edit Cut or Edit Copy. Use Edit Paste, Edit Paste Special, and Edit Paste Link to paste the Clipboard contents into Lotus 1-2-3 or another application in Windows.

Clock A processor contains an electronic pulse generator that is used to transmit synchronised pulses to different parts of the computer for the interpretation and execution of instructions. The synchronisation is set at a speed that determines the computer's CLOCK SPEED. Such clock speeds are measured in Megahertz (MHz). The faster the clock speed, the faster the internal processing speed of the computer.

Closing files Closes the current file and moves the cell pointer to the next open file. When you close a file, Lotus 1-2-3 removes the file from memory but does not delete the file from disk.

COM Computer Output on Microfilm. A form of computer output that offers an effective form of long-term data storage that is both compact and durable. Such output is especially useful as a means of archiving data.

Command An instruction to the computer to perform a given task.

Computer Aided Design (CAD) The use of a computer with graphics software to design through electronic drawing. Main applications areas are in the field of engineering drawing, product design, fashion design and technical drawing.

Control unit That part of the computer's Central Processing Unit or micro-processor which controls movements of data within it.

Corruption A term used to refer to the loss, or corruption, of data. Data corruption is a particular problem when it occurs on a disk. Such corruption can often render data on a disk useless, hence the importance of regular backing-up of data.

Creating a chart A chart is an illustration of data in your worksheet. Charts are effective ways to present data. They can make relationships among numbers easy to see because they turn numbers into shapes (lines, bars, slices of a pie), and the shapes can then be compared to one another.

Criteria These set out the conditions against which records are extracted or deleted from a database. A criteria table has to be set up on Lotus 1-2-3 for this facility to work.

Cursor A small image such as a block or dash on the screen to indicate where data will be entered from the keyboard.

Customising A process of altering a package or environment to suit a particular application. You can customise all SmartIcons in the Lotus 1-2-3 package.

Database The collection, in structured form, of all data representing the basis of information for an organisation's business applications.

DataLens driver A program that Lotus 1-2-3 uses to access data in external database tables. There are different DataLens drivers for each database package.

Date formats In Lotus 1-2-3, dates are represented by values from 1 (the date number for January 1, 1900) to 73050 (the date number for December 31, 2099). A date number does not look like a date unless you format the cell where it appears. After you format the cell, the date appears in the cell, the date number continues to appear in the edit line.

Dedicated computer A computer system set up to perform one specific task or set of tasks. For example, a cash dispenser or an electronic cash till.

Default When offering a choice to users through software, a default value is assumed if no choice is made.

Diagnostic routine A program used to detect errors in either existing software or hardware. Many diagnostic routines will operate in a way that does not interfere with normal operations and is not apparent to a user.

Dialog(ue) boxes These appear during various procedures and require the user to select options.

Disk Drive A peripheral device for storing data generated by the computer's processor and for retrieving data by the processor. Disk drives can contain either floppy disks or hard disks.

DOS (Disk Operating System) Part of the software which is loaded into computer memory and is used to operate the computer system.

Drag To press the mouse button and hold it while moving the mouse.

Drag-and-drop A mouse action allowing you to move or copy data around the spreadsheet.

Driver A part of the Operating System software that is used to control certain peripheral devices.

Edit Undo (SmartIcon) Reverses the effects of the most recently executed command or action that you can undo.

Electronic mail A process of electronically transmitting messages (mail) between computers. Such mail can be stored for future reference.

ERR A special value that either Lotus 1-2-3 generates to indicate an error in a formula or you generate with @ERR. ERR can ripple through formulas: any formula that refers to a cell that contains ERR results in ERR, and any other formula that depends on that formula also results in ERR. When you correct the formula that contains ERR, the results of dependent formulas also become correct. The label ERR is not equivalent to the value ERR.

Field A labelled column in a database or query table that contains the same kind of information for each record. For example, an employee database table may contain fields labelled First Name, Last Name, and Employee Number.

File A collection of records that are related in some way. A stock file, for example, may be a collection of stock records.

File protection A method of protecting files from corruption or accidental erasure. A common way of protecting a file is to write-protect it, which means files can be read but not written to.

Floppy disk A backup medium used to store data.

Flowchart A diagrammatic way of showing functions and sequences of events within a system or sub-system. Flowcharts can take different forms, such as program flowcharts depicting the way a program runs or systems flowcharts showing the way a system works.

Group mode This styles all pages in a spreadsheet in the same manner. When a set of pages, or sheets, are grouped, the alteration of style in any one of them becomes common to all.

Hard Copy Printed output from a computer.

Hardware The computer system, including processor and drives, Cf, Software.

Help Help provides information about all aspects of Lotus 1-2-3. To select a Help topic when Lotus 1-2-3 is in Ready mode, choose a Help command in the Lotus 1-2-3 Help pull-down menu to gain access to broad categories of Help topics, such as Keyboard and How Do I? To select a Help topic using the mouse, point to green text with a solid underline. When the mouse pointer changes to a hand icon, click the mouse button. Using the keyboard, press TAB until the topic is highlighted, and then press ENTER.

Housekeeping A term used to describe the practice of removing unwanted information from disk storage. Good housekeeping speeds up processing and lessens the chance of filling up a disk unnecessarily.

IBM A Trade Name for International Business Machines.

ICL A Trade Name for International Computers Limited.

Icon Pictorial representations of programs and options available for executing or processing. In Lotus 1-2-3 SmartIcon buttons let mouse users click on commonly used commands and macros. These are fully customisable.

Image processing The process of transmitting pictures and images in digitised form.

Input The process of entering data, either manually or electronically, into a computer.

Installing The process of implementing software on to a computer for the first time.

Integer A whole number.

Kilobyte (K) Used to measure data quantity. It represents 1024 bytes of data.

Label-prefix characters The first character in a label entry defines the entry as a label and controls how Lotus 1-2-3 aligns the label in the cell. Lotus 1-2-3 does not display the label-prefix character in the cell but does display it in the edit line when you select a cell that contains a label. Characters: ' (apostrophe): left-aligns labels (default); " (quotation mark): right-aligns labels;

^ (caret): centres labels; \ (backslash): repeats one or more characters across a cell.

Landscape Printing This is when a page is printed across its longest dimension. It is particularly useful when a spreadsheet is wide and occupies only a few rows.

Local Area Network (LAN) A system that connects a number of microcomputers together so that they can share common resources such as a database or printer. While resources can be shared, each computer on a network is still able to act independently of another.

Logging in A method of getting access to a computer's information. Designed for security, the process of logging in requires an operator to enter identification and, normally, an associated password.

Logging out Signing off a system. This should be done whenever an operator has finished work on a computer.

Macro A stored sequence of commands that automates a task.

Menu A list of options to choose from. With Lotus 1-2-3 the pull-down menus offer the first level, with options from each pull-down menu offering further options.

Merge Combining two related files.

Mode indicator An indicator on the spreadsheet that informs the operator about the status of the spreadsheet. For example, READY indicates the spreadsheet is waiting for input while WAIT indicates the computer is busy.

MODEM (Modulator/Demodulator) A device for sending and receiving signals down a telephone line, thereby allowing data communication between computer devices. Such modems will be needed at both ends of a line for data communications to work.

Mouse An input device that interacts with the screen. It moves the image of an arrow or bar around the screen and is used to select options when a mouse button is clicked.

MS–DOS A Trade Name for Microsoft Disk Operating System.

Multiplexer A communications device that receives data from a number of computer devices and then sends such data down

ONE telephone line. There will be a slowing down in data communications transmission from each device as more of them transmit data, but such devices can reduce the costs of data communications quite considerably.

Object An item that can appear in the form of a shape or box on a spreadsheet and be edited, deleted or moved around the spreadsheet. A graph, for example, is a collection of such objects.

Off-line A general term referring to data or part of a computer system being inaccessible. If a printer is off-line it will not print.

Operating System Software that is used to operate the computer and its peripherals.

Operator A term used to describe a person who operates a computer. This is different from a person who programs a computer – a computer programmer.

Optical Character Reader A computer input device that recognises characters, usually in typed form. Such devices can be a considerable labour-saving device when text that has already been typed needs to be entered to the computer.

Password A way of ensuring that only authorised personnel have access to parts of a system. Passwords are only effective if they are kept secret from everyone, excluding authorised persons. Passwords are also set up in a way that ensures different people have access to different parts of the system.

Paste The process of pasting what is stored in the Pasteboard to another part of the spreadsheet, or to a different application altogether.

Peripheral devices Input, Output, and Storage devices of a computer that constitute part of the system hardware.

Protocol Communications protocol is a standard of data communications that tries to ensure compatibility in the way data are communicated across lines.

Range A block of cells referenced by the top left and bottom right cells to give a rectangular block.

Range name A name assigned to a range of cells or a single cell. To see a list of the range names in the worksheet, click the navigator, or press F3 (NAME) when writing a formula or specifying a range in dialogue box.

Relative reference In a formula, a reference to a cell or a range that changes when you copy the formula. A relative reference refers to the location of the data in relation to the formula. A relative reference can be an address or range name. For example, if the formula +A1+A2 is in cell A4 and you copy this formula to B4, the formula changes to +B1+B2. A1 and A2 are relative references, which means that they refer to the values entered in cells two and three rows above the formula. After you copy the formula, the relative references still refer to the cells two and three rows above the formula. If you do not want a cell or range address to change when you copy a formula, use an absolute reference.

ROM (Read Only Memory) A part of the memory in a computer used to store programs in a permanent way. Part of a computer's operating system (e.g. BIOS) is stored on them. Some systems will also have applications software built into ROM.

Run The actual execution of a program.

Scheduling A process of determining the order in which jobs are performed or executed. Such activities can be carried out automatically or by operating, with priorities being set on certain jobs. This tends to be important when working on network systems.

Scroll box The square box in a scroll bar, which you drag with the mouse pointer to make another area of the worksheet or list box visible.

Scrolling The process of running text up the screen when you want to view data past the bottom of the screen. Windows uses scroll bars for just this purpose.

SmartIcon (a registered TM of Lotus Development Corporation) Buttons (icons) in the 1-2-3 window that let mouse users choose commonly used commands and macros.

Software All computer programs, from the operating system to applications software.

Sort A data processing term used when rearranging files into a different order.

Status A signal indicating whether a system is active or not.

Styles Enhancements applied to the current selection using the Style commands. Styles include bold, italics, underlining, frames, lines, colour, patterns, alignment, typeface, type size, and number formats.

Suite A set of inter-related programs. A term often used instead of package.

Tiling windows The method of displaying a number of screens (windows) at the same time by splitting the screen into sections.

Tutorial To learn Lotus 1-2-3 by completing guided tasks, choose Tutorial from the Help pull-down in Lotus 1-2-3. The Tutorial includes eight lessons. They guide you through many kinds of tasks, ranging from entering data to working with a database and creating versions; they also introduce many of the features of Lotus 1-2-3. Each lesson is divided into small tasks, with an explanation describing each task and precise steps for every action you need to take.

Updating The process of altering a spreadsheet or database.

Using Drag-and-Drop to Move and Copy Data Drag-and-drop is a mouse action that lets you either move or copy data. Drag-and-drop does not use the Clipboard. The following instructions explain how to move data using drag-and-drop: 1. Select the cell or range you want to move. 2. Position the mouse pointer on the border of your selection. You know Lotus 1-2-3 is ready to drag-and-drop when the mouse pointer changes from an arrowhead to an open hand: 3. Hold down the left mouse button. 4. Without releasing the mouse button, drag the selection to its destination. While you drag, your selection is represented as a dotted rectangular outline. 5. Release the mouse button when you reach the destination. As in any other move, the data has been removed from its original location and now appears only in its new location.

VDU (Visual-Display Unit) The screen that displays text and graphics.

Window cascade Sizes open windows (Worksheet and Transcript). Arranges them one on top of the other, with just the title bars showing.

Zoom (View Zoom Out/View Zoom In) Decreases/increases the display size of cells. Each time you select Zoom Out, the display decreases by 10% to as small as 25% of the normal size. Each time you select Zoom In, the display increases by 10%. You can set the display size of cells to as much as 400%.